# Creating Universal Truth

## Vincent Janic

*Heart Solutions*
*Victoria, BC*
*Canada*
*Ordering information:*
*www.amazon.com*

Library and Archives Canada Cataloguing in Publication
Janic, Vincent
    Creating universal truth : all is love / Vincent Janic.

ISBN 978-0-9683364-3-4

    1. Spiritual life.  2. Janic, Vincent.  I. Title.

BL624.J44 2011            204            C2011-903581-2

# Table of Contents

Introduction ........................................................... 1
Book 1 Creating Instant Evolution Love in Motion ......... 5
Introduction...................................................7
1 What's Evolved? ....................................9
2 This Is You..............................................13
3 And It Began .........................................17
4 What Was That?....................................29
5 Wow What a Change! ...........................33
6 That Is Awesome ..................................35
7 That's How It Works ..............................41
8 Help You Remember..............................45
9 How We Evolved or Not.........................49
10 How Did We Get Here?.........................55
11 Who AM I? ..........................................63
12 How We Can Be...................................67
13 Certainty of Being................................73
14 Where Are We Going? .........................79
Book 2 Creating Instant Joy Love the Experience .......... 87
Introduction...................................................89
1 Who, What We Are ................................91
2 Show Me Trust......................................95
3 Heaviness Is Gone!...............................99
4 Love You So..........................................105
5 1, 2, 3, To Infinity .................................111
6 What is Faithfulness? ............................117
7 The Three-Headed Snake ......................123
8 All the Prophets .....................................131

9 Being Human .............................................135
10 Don't Taint My Experience ....................139
11 It's All Good ...........................................141
Book 3 Creating Instant Truth Manifesting Our Love.. 143
Introduction..............................................145
1 Help You Believe ....................................147
2 Understanding Your Spirit .....................157
3 Your Little Master ...................................165
4 Technology ..............................................171
5 Land of Confusion...................................179
6 The Three Prophesies..............................186
Acknowledgements ......................................... 190

# Introduction

This book is about the truth that I have come to understand through my experience. What is the definition of truth? Something that has no other answer than what is present to you. This truth may not be acceptable to a lot of people because of the theories that are currently accepted as truth in our society, be it scientific, religious or spiritual.

Two years ago I had an extraordinary experience that resulted in immediate dramatic changes in my life, both physical and mental. Over the last two years my physical and spiritual metamorphosis has continued and now I live the bliss and joy that every child comes into this world with. My understanding of this truth compels me, like the children, to help others experience this love for life. Let me guide you to find this bliss for yourself.

I am an average person and have written about my experience as well as my observation of others who have written or spoken on this subject.

In May of 2009, in about three seconds, I had an experience that took me from a being a dullard to understanding about how everything really works. Then it took nine months to totally understand who and what I am and the process that we all are involved in. I wrote the first book *Creating Instant Evolution* because I wanted to help others know the truth, the whole truth and nothing but the truth! I wrote it in a very simple way because I understand, like no one I've ever seen, read or heard speak about it. It is not merely a musing on the subject.

I have had assistance and guidance in discerning my experiences from my teacher/mother (whom I didn't know, until my experience, had this level of awareness) who has been a naturopathic teacher and healer for over 20 years. Very few people understand these things as she and I do from our experiences.

The questions that spiritual writers, religion and science leave you with are answered in these books. Others give you a piece of the puzzle but none understand it all because theory does not account for experience. The reason I call my books "Instant" is because we are pure thought, pure emotion and pure experience; and the purest and grandest forms of these are instant. Because of my purest experiences, I have developed the ability to receive thought instantly and write in this form. The first book is about my initial experience and then subsequent experiences. This book may seem a little stiff. That's because I was looking for the simplest way to describe things in my own words for your understanding.

This book tells you who we are, shows you with my example and involves you with explanations of how to see these things around us and evolve our Self.

I go into the explanations of holy books, myths and legends, and how we evolved ourselves and devolved ourselves. I explain how to evolve again to a higher level of consciousness if we choose.

The second book is about creating the joy in our life and removing all our fear, doubt and lack of confidence; creating certainty of purpose and passion in our lives and with a few more truths in it. I write these books with clarity, consciousness and frankness because of my experiences. I want people to be released from the control that is put on us by our leaders. I want to help you think, feel and act for yourself—not following the pack and doing what you are told to do.

The third book in this series is about manifesting the love in ourselves and how to change the world; telling you how I did it and reinforcing the principals from Book 1.

A circle has three points and everything is in three parts. You will understand as you read on. I will put in a few other things to clarify some of the theories that exist in our understanding. I want to help change the understandings of the planet—this is the goal of this book.

Remember, choose to think for yourself. Thought is the beginning of everything. Every choice we make creates our life.

In short, I will help fill the gaps left by religious, scientific and spiritual theory and, by showing you my being, feeling and experiencing, help you understand all that we are in relation to everything. With this understanding you can create balance, certainty, purpose and passion in your life and have a choice in the future of your life and this world we love.

# Book 1
# Creating Instant Evolution
# Love in Motion

# Introduction

This book is about our evolution as a human being. It will answer the three questions that most of us on this planet ask at some time in our lives.

Who am I truly?

What is my purpose? and

What happens when I die?

I will take you on a journey of learning how to trust what we are by the example of my death, revival and process of evolution into a new person; I will teach you the principals of the physical universe. This is an honest, frank and truthful, but short conversation about this subject. I will give you the facts straight, as I have come to understand them, and explain them in the simplest form for your understanding; these principals are rather simple and I won't drag things out into many stories and explanations. I live in the Okanagan Valley of British Columbia. This is an important fact that you will need in order to understand later examples.

I am just a regular guy who is not a spiritual writer, scholar, PhD, or someone who has studied these things, and I have found that not very many people know or understand how these things really work.

This knowledge has essentially been around for many thousands of years. Our teachers and masters have taught us, but the knowledge has been changed, twisted and interpreted by those who wish to keep us ignorant. These gifts were destroyed or kept hidden by certain groups, and now fewer and fewer people know or understand correctly.

Many spiritual writers and speakers talk about these things in their books or speak about them. Since the events that happened to me I have listened and read, yet I haven't seen or heard anyone who really knows or understands. They poke around the edges with some of the information but don't connect with the truth. They seem to always leave the listener with only questions and no answers. You cannot have answers or understanding without experience; experience is the greatest teacher. I've seen and heard artists, songwriters, movie and TV producers and especially rock stars, the ones who probably experimented with drugs, write songs with some awareness of the subject, but unless you know what they're talking about in their lyrics you can't understand.

Listen to song lyrics for words like Love, Forget, Remember, Fire, Burning, Shimmering Light, Light of a Thousand Suns, Nothing Matters, Brother, Flame, etc.

# 1 What's Evolved?

I am self employed, work at night and am not connected to the busy daytime world. That gives me quiet time to think and sort through what everything is about; everything is a thinking thing. What do you believe isn't a thinking thing? If it is alive, is it not thinking? Isn't everything alive?

So—what's instant evolution?

Let's start with the definition of "the Evolved": something that has changed or moved forward. The closest thing to a highly evolved being on this planet would be a small child. Someone under the age of five. If you have a small child in your life, a son, daughter, niece, nephew or grandchild, ask yourself what their attitude is towards everything? They know everything, they are fearless, they have no hate; if they fall, they rarely get badly hurt. Why would you say that's true? Are they totally innocent or totally knowing? If a small child is a clear slate, then why do they have an attitude, why a brilliant Mozart or a blind Beethoven?

As an adult we are basically less of everything that a child is emotionally. Are we smarter? No. Less emotional? Yes. Why is that? Our thinking has changed our understanding. Why? What we have been taking in through our life has taken the natural knowledge from us and made us unconscious—asleep to our nature. Rachel, who was 12 months old at the time when I experienced what I experienced, knew. She put her head on my heart and cooed and tapped me on one shoulder as if she understood. She knew and just loved me all the way through my change.

It appears to me that a very high percentage of people on this planet are unaware. Before all this happened to me, I was pretty much the same; I was doing a little seeking of the truth, mostly listening to late night radio. I am writing this in February of 2010 during the 21st winter Olympics. A lot of peace and joy is being felt here in British Columbia, Canada. It has to do with the light of the flame and real pride connecting the people. As well the burden of the so-called daily grind has been lifted from them.

To continue of my previous thought, I began thinking about writing this because I saw a young woman, maybe 20-22 years old, coming into a building early one morning. Her eyes and face were very sad and had a defeated look; I see it in a lot of people. I began to think, "Why is it that I can't help more people feel like I do. Why is it that way?" I'll continue about thought and how important it is to think for ourselves. Other's thoughts are being pumped into us on a continual basis and we are often trying to do too much at once for too long. It confuses the mind. Thinking on my studies of the Bible in the past, I realized that some of the truths are there, but they are hidden in parable and myth and not interpreted for the mass population. Why do I say that now? That is because, since my changes, I think much more clearly and consciously. I encourage you to take time away from all that confusion and allow the mind to flow. That's what the mind does—what thought is, flow. That's how the universe works. It doesn't go in five directions at once. Things spin in one direction, rivers flow, everything flows—that's how your mind works best. By allowing confusion, we devolve our mind or slow our mind down. Therefore, I suggest that we are doing it to ourselves. That then is what I saw in that young woman; someone who had slowed her mind down so much so that it removed a lot of thought and caused less stimulus to act hopeful. This is what's happening to many people today and why we feel the future is hopeless.

I'm here to tell you a much different story, a story of a bright future with understanding of how that will be achieved. Again, what are evolved people? People who know, not just believe they know, what they are and their purpose on this planet and in the universe. If you live in the western hemisphere, you are probably familiar with the Christian Church's Holy Trinity: Father, Son and Holy Spirit. Everything is the Holy triangle, three. Examples are: body, mind and spirit; unconscious, conscious and super conscious. I will elaborate more on that later. Like I said, most people are asleep or unconscious. When we evolve we awaken and become conscious.

What is being conscious? We know that we are body-mind-spirit and have connected with our spirit. You probably heard the term "we are all connected". That's what the change is. We find out that we are one with everything. The All of Everything, the Oneness, the great "I am" or what many on this planet call God/Goddess. What I mean by connected is to be connected with that which is. Does the name "The All of Everything" stir the feeling of emotion in you?

Some people also refer to it as love or the Universal Mind.

Think of it as the largest mainframe computer you can imagine. Some call it the "light" or "the light of a thousand suns!" And we are but a personal computer beside it yet connected to all the knowledge and information of the universe. So, when we know that we are connected to everything, we change or evolve; our whole outlook changes and with that, even physical changes occur, mental as well. This is not something that is easy for the logical mind to understand. So we must look at it from the heart and not the mind. Emotion is the only way to comprehend these things. Love in motion is the flow of it all.

## 2 This Is You

The masters taught us, "We do not die; our body is but a vessel for our mind and spirit, our consciousness and thought." So what is death then? The ending of our corporal body, form or corpse. A highly evolved being would give up their corporal body rather than kill another. That was the case in the masters of masters. As it was given to me from Spirit, we give form life, we are a life form. We are not I, we are mind; the Universal Mind and Spirit which makes us a division of the whole. We have access to all the creative power, energy and abilities on a miniature scale. Imagine a flashlight beside a very large lighthouse; yet you are that lighthouse and the source is the size of Jupiter, the biggest planet in the solar system. An individual Spirit is the engine and thought of any being or thing. We are a light vibrating at a very high speed and are very powerful beings.

We must change our speed to fit any being or thing. That is, slow ourselves down to fit everything in the physical universe. Our brains are connected to the Universal Mind. It, which knew everything conceptually but had no experience, divided Itself into what It was not—fear (dark, heavy energy or the physical); for It is love or light energy or the metaphysical.

This was the first division. This is where the polar opposites or dichotomy was formed, light and dark (energy) zero/one, yin/yang, male/female, love/fear. This polar division (divided by its poles, positive and negative) created, as stated, the physical universes. The Holy Book says after the creation of the heavens and the earth it was dark. And God said, "Let there be light!" This was the second division. The polar opposites, or two, divided by each other again and again until that was impossible. I'll elaborate on this later in the book. These opposites are our essence, thought (knowledge or logic) and emotion (love). These are constants in us. The third part being the physical which is always changing (always change of form).

We created, from the fear, the mythology of evil of all kinds in every faith and culture. We are the experience of That Which Is and that is our whole and full purpose, nothing more nothing less. Every experience is beautiful in its own way. The entire physical universe is the experience. To put it in more understandable terms, God experiences everything through us. We may be a being, star, planet, tree, rock or anything that is in existence. We are the child of God, the only child. It divided Itself trillions upon trillions of times; cell division. We are the universe and we are the process of life! Does It not say, "In the beginning was the word?" The word IS God and was God. Is word not thought made manifest into the physical? The master said, "I am the vine, you are the branches." Some bear fruit and others do not. This is the partnership that we are in. God is the coordinator or manifester, we are the experiencer or spirit. The body or form is the experience. This is our whole nature, three-part being,—mind, spirit, body—the holy triangle or triune, three in one. The masters also said, "Do not worry for it confuses the mind and leads you astray." If you understand what I just explained to you about our true nature then there is absolutely nothing to worry about. Love your neighbor as yourself. If we are a division of the one then they are our brother or sister. Love them unconditionally. I live in awareness, joy and love like a child and I dance and sing because of this awareness. There is not a shred of doubt because of my experience. I live in this as it is the only truth! I have tested all of the principals out, and I live them daily. Many people throughout the ages have experienced what I have but didn't have the guide to explore those experiences and expand their knowledge, so it was denied or slipped away from them. Many poets, artists and musicians have experienced this as well. They expressed it in their work but didn't fully understand, or their work was not interrupted correctly. Poems, songs and paintings hold unexplained meaning. I was lucky to have someone close to me, who had similar but not as profound experiences, guide me in the correct direction. These are the three laws of the universe; just three, not ten. There are no other rules. Remember that we are the only one, there is no right or wrong, good or bad. There is only the experience and each is different and individual.

**Thought is energy** - Thought generates energy. It created the universe in Its form with pure thought energy. It sent out a ball of pure energy which the scientists called the Big Bang. It actually was a singularity that was sent from source to move forward, always forward, creating mass by energy coming together, creating and destroying, always changing. That was the plan nothing more or less. Beautiful and simple isn't it? All thought creates energy in this process. The scientists have discovered that inside each molecule is a small tornado of energy.

**Fear attaches like energy** - That's the mythology. We created the bad and evil. It doesn't exist; it is the opposite of the true reality of love. We cannot experience what we are if we do not know our opposite. The yin and yang of It. This is the divine dichotomy. We have no understanding of what we are because we are experiencing the opposite from what we truly are.

**Love is all there is** - This is the only reality. We are love, the only real thing. Look again at the small child, love is all they know, no fear. The Master said, "Blessed is the small child."

# 3 And It Began

My journey has a little background. In March of 1997, I had an experience of not sleeping properly for a period of about three weeks. I would sleep about two hours and then wake up with a start. My mind would be going very fast and I would not be able to go back to sleep. I managed to get through it and was fine after the three week period. Then in December of 2000, after returning from overseas, I had a conversation in my head with a very authoritative voice. When I mentioned this to some people they advised me to turn to religion. I became a solo student, studying the Bible every day for over four years. That turned off the voice.

Then in the spring of 2005 I got sick again, just like in '97, but this time I had the shakes and went to the hospital for four days where they put me on drugs to sleep. On the drugs, I would sleep for 10 hours a day and then wake up feeling like I had just gone down to sleep for 10 minutes. It felt like my body had slept but my brain was tried. It got worse as I continued taking the drugs, so I threw them out after six weeks on them. I battled what I called "hot head"; the top of my head, ears, and neck were on fire for weeks. Finally by the fall/winter of that year I was able to control it. This is part of the process of change. The consumption of these drugs limits the ability of the body and brain to function correctly. They make people "crazy", or whatever you want to call it, and are dangerous. Just look at the information about all the people they have hurt. After I got myself under control, I shut off my emotions for the next three and a half years so that I could function. A small voice said, "Seek the truth!" So I started seeking the truth on a limited basis, listening to late night radio and watching spiritual speakers on late night TV.

That led to December 2008, when I started talking to local early morning Talk Radio people. We talked about politics in Canada and other things on a regular basis, and I began to awaken from my emotional slumbers. I had made myself dead inside until then; I hadn't even felt much when Rachel was born into our family. In the months leading up to my awakening, I had also reconnected with an old friend I hadn't seen or heard from in about 16 years; we'd grown up together and this connection helped as well. On April 26, 2009, we had a birthday party celebrating Rachel's 1st birthday and my 45th. Ten people showed up including my father and step mother. I'd known that for the last 25 years my father had been suffering from the same thing that I was. So I told him that I'd been working on my emotions, that I was tired of being dead inside. He shrugged and said, "That's good." My wife told me that some people at the party had noticed that I ate a lot of cake and ice cream— by the way I still like it very much. Someone at the party told my wife that people with certain conditions do that.

I didn't like that very much. The rest of the week proceeded as normal except that there was a lot of sugary food left over from the party, so I thought I should finish it up. This was also the week that the H1N1 crisis started. I had a lot of anger about that because I knew it was just another attack by "those people".

Here is where the unusual journey began. It was around 3:00 am on May 2$^{nd}$, 2009. I was working in one of the churches and a song came on the radio that reminded me of my young adulthood. I said to myself, "I had a pretty happy young adulthood, my early to mid twenties. What do I have to feel sorry about? I have a beautiful wife and child!" At that point I decided to be happy! I started to work faster and got out of there fairly quickly and then I moved to the next job and got it done faster.

As I was driving to my next job, I looked at the clock and it wasn't even 5:00 am yet. I got started on the next job, and I said, "Let's see how fast I can move." At first I was confused but then I started moving probably three times any speed I'd seen before. I got to the point which usually would have taken 45 minutes in probably 20 minutes. The speed my hands were moving reminded me of the speed that the 6 Million Dollar Man or Bionic Woman would move. Then I slowed myself down and finished the next part in 30 minutes, which was half the time it generally would have taken. I sat down on a chair and realized that I hadn't been breathing properly and I was high. I couldn't breathe through my nose because it was always plugged. I had to breathe through my mouth to calm myself down. I finished up the kitchen and the rest of the work and then headed home. The blood had rushed to my fingers and they were like balloons. I called my mom to ask some questions and she told me to relax and breathe all the way home.

I went to bed, slept only two hours and then couldn't get back to sleep. When I went to work that night I had lots of energy. My mind was working hard but I didn't feel tired.

The next day I slept about five hours and felt fine so we went out. That night the same thing happened. I slept two hours and was up the rest of the day. Before I really get into this let me say I was 45 years old at the time, all my joints hurt and I became short of breath walking up stairs. I weighed 170 lbs at 5' 10.5". I been working at my profession 25 years so I expected to hurt like that. Plus I wasn't that strong from what I'd been doing. My hearing and eyesight were very bad as well. I'd wake up in a fog and it took a couple hours to get out of it, though I could retain and handle a lot of information.

Here's where the fun began. That day, Monday, May 4th, 2009, all my senses were very good, better than I could imagine. My voice had deepened. I was taking care of Rachel while my wife was at work for a half day. We went to the doctor's office and sat there for 1½ hours waiting to get in.

During that time a group of youths laughed at an old lady for being scared by a doctor bringing her in from the waiting room. From the other end of a very large room, I could hear them whispering under their breath. I said very loudly, "Show some respect." And then we just stared at one another.

The doctor I saw was a young man whom I had never seen before. He was afraid of me because I knew what I needed and was very forthright in my manner. Supposedly he just gave me something to sleep for a six hour minimum. Here's where we really get into it. I took the drugs when I went to bed for a four-hour nap.

When I awakened I thought I was dreaming. There was total darkness around. I said to myself, "I must be out in space," though there were no stars, planets or anything around. Way off in the distance I saw what I thought was the sun and started floating towards it. Seemingly very soon I was on top of it. It looked just like the sun in the movies, an orange colour, not far away. Then I was saying, "I'm going into the Sun." Next I heard a very strong male voice say, "My child, all you have educated yourself on is the Truth." Then I felt myself spinning away slowly, then faster. I said, "What!" Instantly I was back. This time I looked around for a second; everything was pure white with tiny sparkles of a golden colour in it. Then the voice came again, "My child, all you have educated yourself on, is the truth; you may lose the ones you love the most!" Then I started spinning, spinning, and pulling hard, very hard on my solar plexus and back to my body. When I awakened again it was only two hours into my sleep.

I couldn't sleep anymore because my mind was going too fast. I thought at first it was a dream so I managed okay that night. I had some help from my employee friend that night as well. Tuesday May 5th; I had a short turn-around. I woke up around 1:00 pm feeling very foggy and slow. It took about three hours to wake up from the drug. I felt the same as I did four years earlier taking those other drugs. I thought this was supposed to be a sleeping pill only. I finally got fully awake and moving about 6:00 pm. I was at the smaller church around that time and I ran into the pastor. I told him about the fact that I'd been studying religion, but I'd changed to a sort of Spirituality. When I told him of my experience, he really didn't say that much except, "Things happen. It may be a trick of the mind," or something like that. I knew he wasn't educated about any of those things. To him it was all about the word and God as separate from us. We talked about the junior hockey team in town playing a much better team in the final and winning. (This is pertinent to the Journey.)

By that following morning, I was jumping for joy, feeling I knew the Truth. I went to bed between 7:00 and 7:30 am. When I tried to take the drug there was a bad taste in my mouth, but I took it anyway. Stubborn and fearful, my wife told me to get well and other stuff that I shouldn't have listened to. I was home alone.

A couple hours later, I woke suffocating, unable to breathe. I pulled myself out of that situation and then it was a fight for my life. As I now know, that drug was killing my body, and my spirit wanted to leave. The spinning started in my solar plexus. The spinning was moving and it worked its way up. I tried to be calm and when I was calm it stopped moving and calmed. When I said anything three times like, "Oh no, oh no, oh no," it started spinning again, up my chest and into my arms, I had no control over my arms or hands. I tried to walk, got to my phone and called my mom. I left a message, "I need help this drug is killing me."

My hands got to the point of spinning. I managed to stop the spinning, got downstairs, found some paper and started writing about what I thought this drug was doing to me. I was fighting to stay awake. Finally, on the living room floor, feeling like I was falling off to sleep, I asked, "Lord, please help me," three times. When I had gone to the light, I knew that it was the consciousness of the universe and I was one with it, but I still had my individuality. As I faded away, as if to go to sleep, I felt a force rising up in me. It started low and rose. Like the power of a freight train it almost lifted me off the floor. With the roar of many lions, my mouth was opened the size of a lion's mouth or a hippopotamus' mouth; then I bowed down on the floor! The energy that came through blew out all limitation and expanded my body's capacity in all areas.

"Fuck the drug companies!" was the first thing that came out.

Then I heard, "My child your will is so strong!"

I said, "This isn't the Mount of Olives is it?"

"I come when you call my name."

So I walked over stiffly to the paper and wrote "I am the LORD your GOD" in very large letters, "Trust, go with the flow, just do it, do not heed the false prophets."

I would come in and out asking questions and getting answers. Some of the writing was very large, when the emotion was high. I remember, "Tell the M to stop the killing!"

Spirit wrote five pages of automatic writing through me, and then I got dressed and phoned some people. I didn't know why at the time. Spirit called the small church and left a message with Carin, the office manager, saying, "Carin, this is the Lord your God. Vincent needs help. Please call him. There's a paper here the pastor needs to see." Then Spirit called the other church, talked to the pastor there and basically said the same thing, laughing and joking with the minister.

Finally I went upstairs to bed. My mom called and Spirit answered and said, "Mother, Vincent can't come to the phone, he's been through a lot and he's out right now." I was there but I wasn't, it had taken over my body. My mother knew what was going on. She never told me the truth for a long time, I had to discover it on my own. We must understand what we are on our terms.

I asked about the local hockey team and it said, "Humans." I then asked to cleanse my body. I could feel my teeth very smooth like they were brand new or something.

I woke about 4:00 pm and prepared to go to work. When I was eating my mouth would open very wide. This lasted for four days. To this day it opens wider than it did before.

I called the pastor of the big church and told him to ignore that call because I was on some drugs. He hadn't come like we asked anyway. That night I got my friend/employee to help out and while at one of the buildings, I showed him the five pages of automatic writing. He looked a little shocked, but wasn't really surprised by it.

In the morning I finished at about 8:00 am at the big church, so I went over to the small church and talked to the pastor who was in at that time. I was still fully aware, my voice was still very deep and said to him and Carin that I was on those drugs, but I had the fire within. I told him about a climber who had it and didn't wear protective clothing to climb mountains. The look in his eyes was that of fear,. I could see it, I can still see it.

I went to meet with the funeral director downtown to sign a new cleaning contract with that funeral home. I had known him for a few years. While I was waiting by the thermostat I noticed that it read 68°F and I was freezing. My friend said later that there probably was some dead person hanging around, they tend to do that in funeral homes. As well you feel a lot of hot and cold in this state, mostly in your head, knees, elbows, feet and hands because they are the easiest points of exit for your extra energy. So I talked to the funeral director and I told him that I was changing at my age. He was wide eyed, considering he's the same age as I am. Friday I called a healer and made an appointment to see her Saturday. She talked to me about ascension. Friday morning I called the radio guys again in my super conscious voice. They were talking about the hockey team. I said, "Will beats skill." The crowd on Saturday needs to use that energy to carry the team. They had been badly beaten in the last two games.

I went for two more days with two hours of sleep each day. Yet I had so much power and strength I didn't know how to handle it. On Saturday, May 9th, I came home at 8:00 am and made love to my wife. It was so powerful she couldn't believe it.

I slept about 50 minutes, awoke around 9:50am and could not get back to sleep I was so high.

I went downstairs and played with Rachel. After my wife called my sister, she wanted me to go to the hospital, but I told her I couldn't use any more drugs, they would kill me. I was totally aware, I could hear everything from upstairs, the conversation, the child, and when I talked to my sister, my voice was strong.

She asked, "What's wrong?"

I said I didn't know, but I did.

I was lying on the bed. My wife was standing by the door and was going to call for an ambulance. I had the thought to stop her and immediately I teleported across the room and said, "Whoa." She looked freaked out.

I told her, "Let's just go see the healer and get this under control, everything will be fine." I drove to the healer's house and felt fine, strong. We got there and I talked to her about things and I managed to be calmed right down.

She did her treatment and after we talked about calmness and flowing water. Then she made me burn the paper with the automatic writing on it. She showed me some skills on how to balance my energy. When I got home I slept for maybe four or five hours. Then I started to send excess energy back to the earth. She had told me make my finger and toes like roots and the energy would filter back. She said, "Tell it to go back to the earth, to the core."

At first it was slow, then I pushed and the energy went out like a direct current. It was very strong. I did that for an hour or so but still didn't feel right. I went to the other room at about 8:00 pm and tried to sleep. Then the scent that she was using in the healing session came back into my nose, and I started to breathe, back, back, back, as far as you can image and further, it was like I was breathing to the back of my head. Then, with my eyes closed, a laser-like light started spinning and removing my negative thoughts. The thoughts were coming fast and being erased by the light, each layer of thought. I yelled out, "YES, YES, YES," until it was all cleared and then I started speaking a singsong language that I didn't know, maybe Chinese or something else. That went on for about three minutes or so; my hands were moving as I talked as well.

At the end of all that I said, "I am that I am." It just came out.

I turned over and said, "No, how's that possible?" That's what is called a clearing.

## 4 What Was That?

There was a lot of confusing information in that last chapter so let's analyze it so it can be better understood. With the knowledge that I've acquired over the last nine months, I've evolved to the point of full understanding of those events.

I learned that the sleep disorder that happened to me back in 1997 is part of the process of awakening and happens to a lot of people. I had it explained to me like this; the start that you got was the energy of your spirit returning to your body and you noticed it then because your body's metabolic rate has changed. The solution is to adjust your energy, or eat foods such as raw vegetables, fruits and water; that will bring your body back to where it was and needs to be, to be in balance. Do not self medicate with sugar, alcohol, or drugs; all drugs including caffeine and nicotine. These are observations not recommendations. Remember life is about opportunity and choice, always choice in all situations. When I decided on May 2nd of last year to be happy, that was my choice, but the principal here is this; all states of being are a state of mind; meaning there is no try, just do it or be it.

My understanding of the experience of going to the light is that Universal Mind says, "You will know I am communicating with you through pure thought, pure emotion, and pure experience." The purest and grandest is always the way Universal Mind communicates with me. Remember, I didn't go through any doors; there were no dark places, no angels, no dead relatives, just straight communication. These things are illusions. I was surrounded by total peace, love, and knowledge. When I died the energy that rose up in me was my spirit re-energizing my body, through and through of that which IS. It's always our choice to leave, not Spirit's. If we ask it will do what it can to jump start our body. In this case, the body was overdosed on the drug and it couldn't take anymore; so it blew out the drug or blew the breaker in the drug and carried me for three days until my body recovered. Remember that everything is energy so everything has a breaker in it. I haven't been sick since because of what this taught me or I remembered. Every time I feel like I may get sick or have a virus in me I blow it out. Even in November 2009 when H1N1 Virus was very strong, I got it out. It took a big effort. My contacting the pastors was to be witnesses to my condition and they really couldn't deny it, could they? After all this is supposed to be their line of work.

As far as the junior hockey team and my calling up the radio guys saying, "Will beats skill," I'd been following them the whole playoff, had learned about consciousness and thought transfer and I was practicing on them. Unknown to me at the time, because as young men their focus wasn't as good as it might have been, ı working to increase their focus and it was working, until the finals when I got "sick" so to speak. Here the fans are fair-weather fans. They get easily perturbed and turn negative. So I asked the fans to carry them to victory in game six and they did. That's how mass consciousness works. Using the thought energy of the masses helps others get the result they need or want. This can be negatively used as well and is often unconscious.

The last part was of the clearing; clearing is the cleansing of the negative thoughts or memories from the brain so our filter is clean. In other words, our brain is a microprocessor or a computer. It operates body functions as the computer operates programs. Also it receives direction from a disc (Spirit) and outside internet (Universal Mind). So it is a receiver and transmitter of information. This information is thought which is energy, and we are receptacles of that thought energy.

The hot and the cold is extra energy finding a way out of the body. The head, ears and joints are the easiest route out of the body, and this was a very heavy dose of energy to re-energize my body after my death!

The teleportation is the moving through space at the speed of thought. I was totally aware of what I was at that time. That's the way highly evolved people move large distances when they need to move fast. You may have heard of highly evolved people in vehicles that move very fast and in very odd ways; moving in 90 degree angles without stopping. This is how they do it.

The comment about religious groups killing in the name of God is brought up because this is the highest form of blasphemy. If we understand we are one, then the killing of any one or thing in the name of God has no merit.

# 5 Wow What a Change!

When my clearing was completed, I felt the membrane between the two halves of my brain had melted; my abilities changed instantly (instant evolution). My left side, which was lazy and I wasn't very capable with, had became stronger. It improved immediately to probably 60% of my right side instead of 20 to 30%. My memory and the ability to retain information better was instant. My strength increased by at least 30%. My fingernails instantly went from cracked, chipped and weak, to perfect, strong and sharp. All my joints were pain free. My breathing and my lung capacity increased by at least 30%.

My mind became much stronger, and I basically walked on air. You know when they say you are on cloud nine, well that's how it feels all the time. I feel everything. My touch is so soft, the stiffness is gone and my flexibility is that of a very fit16-year-old boy, even more fit than I was at 16. After a few months my entire body has been renewed, restored and reinvigorated, like that of a 17 to 20-year-old young man. I have no problem getting 15-17 hours of work done on a regular basis. Sleep is always, always required as it is the most important thing for everyone! I sleep like a worry-free child.

Also the energy is always running through me. The fog that I had in the morning is gone and my eyes are the eyes of a young child, milk white and alert, not saggy and drooping down. The first words that came to me as this happened were, "I'm evolving." I feel awesome.

# 6 That Is Awesome

Let me explain energy for a minute. We are light beings, that's why I was brought back. That light and energy being wants to experience the physical and through the form of physical it does so. Like I said at the beginning, we are a division of ALL THAT IS, and ALL THAT IS experiences everything through us. The scientists say that they detect a radiant energy in the universe, one they believe is a residue of the big bang, but as I said before it is life, it is the process through which everything is!

And it is the essence of our own being and all beings and things in the universe; our engine so to speak. This energy is all around us, in us, in everything, all of space, planets, all life; that's what is....IT!! Some call it the field but do not understand it. I sense this as the flow of energy though my body. If I want more energy, I turn my hands up and pull it in. If I'm over energized it will leave through my feet, hands and ten fingers, ten toes.

Our number system is based on this. All is divine, hands and feet are the most divine aspects of the body–10 fingers and toes. Then there is the trinity of body, mind and spirit. Divide 10 by 3 and you get 3.33 to infinity. Are you getting the holy triangle yet? I'm trying to be simple, straight and understandable. It feels like a tingling, like when your hand or foot is coming back again after it has fallen asleep. That's the sort of feeling. You see stars in front of your eyes when you bump your head. Those stars are your light coming through. For another example of energy try this; rub your hands together then hold them as close as possible together without touching. Do you feel a tingling? Now pull them apart and as you bring them together you will feel a field of energy there. You are constantly sending and receiving this thought energy. Remember the first law—thought is energy.

Now I'll continue the journey. After the clearing, I noticed all the physical changes, especially my breathing and strength. It took me a couple of weeks to adjust to the change in the amount of pressure that I needed to apply. I was used to using a certain pressure to apply on things: closing doors, lifting and throwing. I would bump something and it would break or fly an unusually long distance. I recall closing a cupboard door and hearing some glass break from the force. It was awesome, but a bit of an adjustment. Since I mostly work alone it was probably much easier for me than for others who have dealt with the change. Let me say that I have been very lucky in this regard because my mother had this experience 20 years ago, knew what to do and guided me in the right direction. Some who have experienced this do not achieve this level of awareness because of the negative programming that all of us have. Some can have more sensitivity than others. For example psychics have their own path. We all must respect each others' paths. I remember about a week after this happening going to visit former neighbours saying, "It's all true, brother and sister." I was jumping for joy. I recall in June going to the dentist for a cleaning and got an X ray done that showed some of my root channels growing back in. I said to the hygienist, "I been working on my teeth."

She said, "Whoa that's over my head."

My broken tooth was still the same, so I said, "I have to work on that I guess." I will tell you more later in that regard.

As I was saying, the energy was flowing and I was adjusting to my new body. Mom said, "You should read *Conversations with God Book 1* by Neale Donald Walsch." I don't have much time to read, but around the 1st of July I found it in the small church library. I read the first two chapters and I was good with it. It confirmed things I knew were true. We know everything; we just need to remember as I said earlier.

I was good with just being and experiencing, yet Mom said to read more. When I had time, I did read more. Here is where I started to learn, or remember as Spirit says. The 1st Law is "Thought is Energy". How do we get what we want? Ask for it, right? You've heard others say this stuff for centuries and centuries, but nowhere before had I read those lines in the book that said, "All things are Energy and thought is Energy." The key to unlocking the power and creativity of the universe is understanding that you=Spirit and the Universal Mind=thought-word-action or deed. The first key is prayer or focused thought. The second key is that we must ask in gratitude; that is to ask as if we have already received it. Third, our supplemental thought, our thought behind the thought, must be that of no doubt that we have received it. The religions say believe and receive, but if we don't ask we won't receive. Some say God will provide and has, but we need to ask for what we really want. The warehouse is being depleted and we need to refill it. Nothing lasts forever without being replenished. The Universal Mind is like a copying mechanism so if we follow these things we will receive.

This book is about helping others. All books are examples of things that we might follow. Like the Master said, "Help the fisher's fish. Give them a net or a pole to fish with," or something close to that. Spirit wants us to use our own thoughts and words.

Okay back to thought-word-action. I read that and said, "Okay, I tried it a few times, but it didn't work." Then later in July (not sure of the date), Saturday afternoon the fires started over on the other side of the Lake. It was very windy that afternoon. I was headed to work about 4:00 pm, and I was listening to the radio. The fire that started on one side of the highway had jumped and was heading to the other side where there are many houses. I asked a few times for the wind to die and help the fire fighters. Not that long after another fire started, than another, and then finally the wind died. On Sunday I had a job to do and asked for more help for the fire fighters. A rain storm popped out of nowhere and cooled down the first two fires. By Tuesday morning the people were allowed back to their homes. I called the radio guys on Monday morning and said, "You see, prayer does work! The rain came out of nowhere; I wasn't sure yet if it was my asking or not." I was still in the afterglow of the change and just wanted to experience it all. On the 15th of July, I talked to my sister about our conversation in May and gave her a message that I was fine to take her for her birthday on the Sunday. We spent the day visiting in Armstrong and on our way back home, the Terrace Mountain fire exploded (the third one). It was small and a long way from everything, but some people had to be evacuated from their homes. It got very hot after that. I had been playing golf on the Sundays in the heat, had a lot of energy and was playing well. I hadn't played as well since I was a young man. I would draw energy from the sun. Because my body had not yet fully recovered I would lose focus by the last few holes and then things would not go well.

Since the clearing, I'd been following the healer's advice about drawing and sending back energy; trying different avenues and making roots with my hands and feet. First it was the Earth receiving and sending, then the Moon, then the Planets smaller to bigger. (Jupiter was very powerful as the summer passed.) I kept doing that; the sun was really affecting me. Then the August long weekend came and we planned to go out of town. I worked until 2:00 am on the Saturday, slept two hours, then drove eight hours to the East Kootenays and felt fine. I played golf on Sunday. I received a call from my friend/employee about the jobs he was doing. He told me the heat and smoke were very bad that weekend and we noticed that the smoke was hanging around in the valley.

On Monday I played 16 holes but couldn't finish as we had to leave by 1:00 pm to get back home to work later that night. I drove 6½ hours back (that way was shorter), slept 1 or 2 hours, and worked 6 hours that night. This is another example of my mental Energy. I was quite intoxicated by the strength at the time. Also, by this point, time had become non-existent for me. That is, you spin so fast that time doesn't exist. There are those who believe that it's time that speeds up, but it is us. And time does not exist; it is a human construction to measure the spinning of the Earth through space. Remember thought—word—action first. Think it—say it—then trust it will happen.

Manifestation is the action of the Universal Mind. Also, remember that the thought must be in gratitude as if we have already received it and without any doubt. We cannot trick our mind. We are that process of the universe; we are a partner in that process, mind and spirit, which gives the body, the universe, life. The body is the experience, always remember that. This is a self-truth book, the universal truth, to help you see the truth in you.

# 7 That's How It Works

On Tuesday, the 3rd of August, the smoke was terrible where I was working. As I said, my lung capacity had changed and it was really bothering me. By Thursday night I was getting upset with it. That night, I watched the evening news and the weather forecast was for a slight shower. The heavy rain was supposed to be in the Kootenays, we were supposed to get maybe 1 mm of rain. I was in my truck around 10:00 pm, in front of one of my jobs and I prayed this prayer, "Thank you Father/Mother for helping the firefighters in this forest fire. Don't allow this storm to pass over. Make it pour. Make it pour. Make it pour!" I said that with a very open heart and with gratitude and belief. It started raining and it got heavier as the night passed. It rained all night and most of the day Friday. I watched the newscast on Friday. They said it rained fairly heavily all over but at the base of the fire it rained 50 mm or 2". It was under control quickly thereafter and the fire was basically never a problem again that summer. The residents returned home; mop-up continued until sometime in September.

A couple weeks later, I was working on a Thursday night; I hadn't continued reading the book yet. I asked myself, "How did I manifest spirit?"

I started thinking or remembering, "What did I do?"

"Please, Lord, help me," I asked three times and this was revealed.

I started seeing the groups of three. Sun, Moon, Earth; blue, green, white. Most of the primary elements are three. $H_2O$ and $CO_2$. Most star systems are three or a multiple of three or a division of three: the 12 disciples of Jesus. I went on with these numbers. I saw The Holy Triangle, The All of Everything!

Another incident that happened in August was that I had a very clear dream that I appeared to be observing. I went by a house and three men were talking. It turned into an argument. The one man took out a sword or machete and killed the other two and then himself. I saw everything. There was a lot of blood. Later an older man was crying and cleaning up the mess. It appeared to be a time when there were no people in authority to come around and check out the incident. My teacher (my mother) told me this was another life that I lived and remembering it is part of the process of awakening which can be very traumatic.

As well, one afternoon I woke up in my body and my body was stiff. I was also lying beside my body in spirit. I said, "He sees us," and I jumped back into the body with a big jerk or jolt. My neck snapped pretty hard. I guess I misaligned getting back into my body, it happens. Another dream I had that day was pretty intense too, but all I remembered was that I was a female member in a royal court.

Before we go on let me explain my use of "Universal Mind". When I use Universal Mind I am referring to the

All and the Everything, the Ebb and the Flow. Universal Mind is both male and female or the absolute.

S.E.X. Synergistic Energy Exchange. Have you ever had sex and felt the energy when climax occurs? The energy that flows through you comes out the top of your head? The top of your head is where Universal Mind communicates with you. I get a heat or burning in my crown energy centre (Chakra). When this happens you may find yourself screaming three words, usually something like, "Oh yeah oh," "Oh my God," "Oh f—k yeah," or "Oh s—t yeah," and it's pretty universal. What happens is your energy centers line up and the energy flows from your feet to the top of your head. That's an example of the exchange of energy that I feel all the time but on a slightly lower level. I can bring it up just by allowing the energy to flow in and it can get very good! (Some need to meditate for long periods to reach this point. It only takes me a couple of minutes.) We are attracted to the energy that we had as a small child, or the unity of the one, of the Universal Mind, but we repel Universal Mind to keep our individuality. Universal Mind is the whole from which we come, the one, but we must experience the opposite to know who we are. Have you heard the phrase "Opposites Attract"? It's a natural attraction that only happens when the opposites are apart, again, being separate to know who we are. That's the whole point of the physical universe; the ebb and flow, the moving forward, always changing; the simplicity of it all.

This is also referred to as the divine dichotomy, that which is and is not, the divine or not, light or dark, the space and the space in between. The ancients called it the isness of is and is not. Examples of this are the beauty of something and the ugly side of it; a rose with the beauty and the thorns, the beautiful woman or man who is cruel; the institution that builds beautiful buildings but teaches ugly values or standards. The most noted of this dichotomy in nature would be a fire, storm, hurricane, or tornado; the beauty of the form with the destructive result that it leaves. These things are very well used in legends and myths.

Some writers have spoken of living in the moment. That's because the moment is all there is, no past or future exist at that moment. So live in it; the eternal moment of now that's all that exists. Don't make promises you can't keep because everything is always changing. Time doesn't exist, it is a human construct (as I said back at the end of the last chapter). Everything is spinning: Earth, solar systems and galaxies. It is a matter of turning from light to dark. No time actually passes but our minds have been conditioned to believe it does so we age as well.

## 8 Help You Remember

In September I wanted to play more golf, so I asked for mild weather, between 25 and 30 degrees Celsius, until the end of the month and I said thank you for the mild weather until the end of the month. Well that's what we got. I couldn't play but it was very nice. Remember to focus on what you want as if you already have it. It may seem trivial; every time I go from one place to another I ask for green lights all the way. I almost never have to wait for the light any more than slowing down for a few seconds, and I rarely have to come to a complete stop. How does this help me? It saves time. Universal Mind wants you to experience the best, and Universal Mind experiences what you experience.

I will tell you about another incident that happened one morning in October when I was driving home from work. I relaxed my mind, which I rarely do, and I fell asleep at the wheel. My mind yelled at me to wake up! It had never happened before yet on the same trip it happened again. I woke and my body had responded before I knew what happened; it hit the brake as hard and as fast as I've ever done. I was a foot away from going into a deep ditch. These things are an example of how my body and spirit have melted together consciously to protect my life, in addition to all that Spirit did to keep me from dying last time.

During the period from October to December my body was being restored—rebuilt—reinvigorated; it was like going through puberty again. I had things happening to me like I was 14 or 15 again. At the end of October I said a prayer to fill the watershed of this area. I said three different prayers, not one prayer three times. In early November, a lot of rain and snow fell on the south coast of British Columbia and Washington state. Not that much made it here, so I was wondering why. I asked my teacher and she said, "Be more specific." I changed my prayer to, "Give us a warm winter with lots of precipitation in the mountains of the interior to fill the watershed." The snow started falling in the mountains around here. It continued through December and January. I heard words coming from the ski resorts like "fantastic" and "epic". Then it stopped snowing. What I figured out was that the people around here got worried. Worry is holding a negative thought and pushes what you want away. The principal is that what you give away, or allow the universe to deal with, comes back to you 10, 20, 30 fold. I trusted, but the mass consciousness didn't and they held the thought or worried.

What you hold is pushed away from you. Do you understand how that works? All things are thinking beings or things. I'm telling you these examples so you can learn and believe in yourself. Follow me and you will have life; that is, follow my ways and you will have the best life possible. Those were the master's words. Remember everything is about you and who you are. Everything is an example, all our holy books, myths and legends etc. I'm repeating myself on purpose to bring home the point. Focused, concentrated thought is the key to everything.

You may say, "If anyone can do that they may use it in a bad or selfish way." As I said before, we must be grateful and have no doubt in our mind.

When we are grateful and free of doubt it is very difficult, if not impossible, to do anything in a selfish way because, whenever we evolve, our thought patterns change to a selfless way of doing things. Although it is all about self, we are all one and our being only wants the best for us (We are one with all.) We become a person who lives in honestly, integrity and truth which in turn makes our heart open to all and, in that case, we wouldn't do a selfish thing. I'm not saying everyone who evolves does this but with an ungrateful mind the ability to create will be limited.

## 9 How We Evolved or Not

So let's get to it; how do we evolve our minds to a higher level? As I told you, when I changed I went through a clearing, the layers of negative thought were removed. How did our brains get programmed with this negative thought? I'll show you how so you can understand how our filter is clogged and how we can free ourselves to think clearly again. I'll show you what is done and why I don't condone any of these institutions. We are minimized, marginalized and mechanized.

1. Minimized: this is done by the teaching of religions. The history of this goes back many thousands of years, before the ice ages, when we were a highly evolved society which knew the truth about ourselves. The God and Goddess were all love and we knew our role in the universe fully and completely. The God of this age (present day) was created and nurtured by men who wanted power and control over others. That is the God we have been taught about and those teachings have resulted in all the things that we are afraid of today. As a small child we know what we are, and where and why we are here. That is educated out of us with religion and other minimizing tactics, today it may not be religion but those values have been passed down. They teach us that

we are less than we are; the fallible human with only one life and no way out except death.

2. Marginalized: We are told that if we have any of these traits, free thinking, a non-traditional concept of God, that we are on the wrong side or crazy or many other unflattering labels. In the Holy Books these are described as the black artists: psychics, seers, witches, warlocks etc. and in the legends these people are always marginalized as wizards, old hags or witches. We are taught that we don't want to deal with them or we'll be mislead or worse. These are the free thinkers, the free spirits.

3. Mechanized: We've been turned into non-thinking beings fit only to work and consume. How was that done? In the early part of the industrial revolution the church and state were losing their control of the individual, no more serfdom. In Western Europe and North America young lads were beginning a life at the ages of 13 or 14, running businesses, doing things in society that adults do today. They had good sense and functioned well in society. In the 1850s education was invented; not the old standard of the church or tradesman but Government Education built around the military model of memorizing and remembering things that had no real day to day value. Reading and mathematics were always taught by institutions. This was a way mechanizing the workers, turning them into machines to do certain tasks and only those; not to think but to do. This also turned them into perfect consumers for the products. Things have not really changed.

What that does to our brain is block it up with information that is not true, and we are unable to receive knowledge from the Spirit, which knows everything, and the Universal Mind, which is the all-knowing everything. So what did I say here? Your filter is blocked with negative information which is untrue and conflicts with the true knowledge that you receive from within. That causes confusion, doubt and lack of confidence in what's true. Therefore it blocks up the receiver in your brain, layer after layer after layer. The things we knew as a small child conflict with all the other information.

How do we clean out? As I said before, everything is thought—word—deed, and the universe was created in three steps: conceive (thought)—create (word)—experience (deed). We are the experience, as I also said before, so reverse the typical process of doing in order to experience. Whatever you want to experience—conceive that thought, speak or think the words and then watch the experience unfold. In other words, think what you want to experience. Every experience starts with a thought—conceive the thought, create the words and then experience it. Remember how I thought back on May 2nd, 2009 I wanted to be happy so I made those thoughts my experience? It happened very quickly, but I panicked because of the fear in my brain that was put there by previous thought and experience. So remember that if we conceive a thought and focus on that thought momentarily and then let it go, it will become our experience. We are the created and the creator. We cannot not be.

Think light positive thoughts constantly until all doubts are replaced with light, belief and total confidence in the truth. The knowing and not knowing is the divine dilemma. But by reinforcing those thoughts on a daily or constant basis we will overcome that dilemma. There are ways to adjust when the change starts. One is by changing our diet. To adjust your vibration, change to all raw food. To adjust your energy, seek assistance from an energy healer like I did; some do not even totally understand what I do. This may take a few weekly sessions.

Like the Holy Book says, build your house (life) on a rock. Nothing can affect you if you do, because you know All That Is. The holy books are not all bull, about 30% is truth. They had to put the natural truths in to keep people coming but they play the positive/negative game with our mind to control us. I had this confirmed to me by a former pastor. Always remember we are an everlasting energy and light being. The universe spins in one direction—forward and always positive—it creates and destroys (we are always changing form; we give form life) with light, energy and the divine (us) always and forever. It says, "I am the beginning and the end." That's what spins (a circle, everything is a circle). That's the universe always spinning.

So let's talk about the signs that you are changing. First step your sleep may be interrupted for a short time as mine was, sleeping only two hours. Second your thoughts will be racing. Some things that you may not know come in; in dreams as well. Third the speed at which you vibrate will change. In my case, I started moving a lot faster and lighter. Your strength will increase, things are not as heavy for you. Those were the times when, whether you were stressed or happy, you moved easily through tasks without effort?

## 10 How Did We Get Here?

I have a few more examples to give you and I'll get to
that later. First we'll talk about how we evolved the way
we have, why the earth is changing and how. Most of the
education that most of us have received in our lives tells
us that there were no truly evolved humans on this
planet until fairly recently. That's the story because the
evidence doesn't exist right? Well that depends on who is
looking and what story they want to be told.

There are hundreds of books out that talk about these
subjects in greater detail. I'm going to give you an
overview of these things. And some of my information is
different. As some cultures that exist, or did in the recent
past, have told us, we are the fifth civilization of humans
to rise on this planet. The Holy Book speaks of the
beginning and they believe that was less than 10,000
years ago. Well that may be this one but others came
before that time—much before.

We know that at least three million years ago we were
intelligent enough to come out of the trees, so we just
existed from then until now? Maybe not. I've heard that
we had a first rising of a society, which I spoke of to you
earlier, who lived in concert with the land and knew
everything. That was over 200,000 years ago. These
people lived a very long time. The earth was perfect for

all species to thrive. It had a perfect climate worldwide and the land masses were connected together in relatively the same position as today, not close to the equator like the scientists say. How could the planet spin when all the weight was in the centre? It wasn't!

Think of the evidence. They have found tropical vegetation and dinosaur bones on Ellesmere Island in the Arctic. Now if that's the case, how could the climate not be tropical? The holy books speak of a "firmament" around the planet, or cloud cover, water vapor which created a tropical climate throughout. That water vapor was there from the beginning of life so it could support all forms of life. The water came from the sky. Green (plants), blue (ocean) and white (cloud, not snow) are the colours of the earth.

This was there at the beginning of the human civilizations as well. It supported an easy social life where everyone could easily survive and not have a struggle. When they needed something they asked. If it was a dry year for example they asked for rain, etc. People lived in perfect health and for very long periods. That was accomplished by self healing methods and eating the fruits of the land. As I spoke of earlier, the spirit healing the body.

As the civilizations changed and developed higher technology they moved away from their connection with the earth as we have. Each society has done their damage to the earth, some less and some much more. Each time a society fell, the earth repaired, restored and renewed itself. But the last society did the some very bad damage to the atmosphere, causing an ice age that lasted a long time; we are only guessing the length. They built underground cities and they are still there. Many people talk about them all over the world. We are the descendents of these people; we came to the surface at that time. Remember H.G. Wells' time machine? This is a reference to that time. We have evolved and devolved many times. Many cultures have legends of coming out from the underworld or even the hollow earth theory.

I've heard and know the other evidence of these periods. Some today know the knowledge of the ancients, but do not share it with the masses. My point here is that truth is not what we have been told in all regards. Remember our ancients' cultures and their so-called backwards ways. They had invented things like a battery and a computer of sorts. These things are documented. Where did they get the knowledge that came to them? The building of the ancient monuments, where did that knowledge come from? We cannot duplicate those building techniques today; we can come close but not the fit or the strength of those buildings. If so we would be using them since some are much superior to our methods. As well they had myths that are not explained: Hercules, Sampson, where did these men get their strength? Hercules was supposed to be the son of Zeus! Who was Zeus? He was the head god and all the other gods were under him. Sound familiar; "Ye are gods," it is written. That's what I've been saying. We are the division of the one, right? And what about Sampson? He was fully human wasn't he? Yet he could take out 13 men at once and he brought down the temple on all who were in it.

Where did his strength come from? The same source that I have been talking about. Take a look at all the old legends from all cultures. The ones who were true of heart and mind always got what they wanted. Our modern myths, the superheroes, what is their trait? Super strength. But they were honest, lived with integrity and spoke truth. They never used their power to kill except when absolutely necessary as a last resort. With great power comes great responsibility. We can all be that way and create a better world. Keep in the mind that the opposite also exists and this power can be used negatively.

Back to the pantheon of gods, who were they? Each had their specific area that they were in charge of. I read a book the other night in which the author said we humans are generalized in our views. Specific things escape us all though these things are right in front of all of us. Generally speaking we tend to over generalize things and to not see the specifics of things. Now what I am getting at here is that we have had this knowledge in front of us all the time; in our history, myths, legends and holy books. But it's another example of how the truth has been twisted or changed. Again, the reason we cannot see these things is the programming that we've had done to us, systematically changing the way we see things, especially specifies. I now see them everywhere every day. They are very obvious to me; a clear brain leads to a clear outlook.

In my estimation, the pantheon of gods was a council of elders, masters or teachers in the past who taught how to create things in a certain area. Even then they had some of that knowledge, but it was lost. I'll tell you later where I think this should be used.

As I was saying about the earth, she has repaired herself many times. Think of the beginning, how the planet was a molten mass with no life. We worry about things today but remember we have been coming in since life was possible on this planet from the small one cell organisms to plants to dinosaurs to mammals. This planet is a very strong and alive being. She has seen it all. She built up stores of carbon from the days of the volcanoes as a warehouse on which to draw. Carbon is the building block of life. Always remember that any high school biology student knows that. So why is it now being called pollution! It's anything but. As I said earlier, this planet has survived more than you can imagine, building, rebuilding, restoring itself just as we do.

After the last Ice Age, after our ancestors had nearly destroyed the atmosphere with their technology and lack of stewardship of the earth, she began restoring herself and now she has started rebuilding the atmosphere so we and all others on the planet can live an easier life. Her will is stronger than any of us know and we cannot stop it, just help out. We've been helping out over the last couple decades. Carbon in the atmosphere is a source of life and burning of trees supports that. Yet now we're being encouraged to cut back in burning wood. However, the process of rebuilding the earth is underway and only good can come of it now. Remember, no thing dies, it only changes form.

As for rebuilding the structure of the earth, all these earthquakes are mostly a release of negative energy that we have been putting into the earth. She is releasing it all at a very strong rate of late because people are letting out so much negative energy. Look around at the mental state of the earth, it has to go somewhere and she cannot contain it all. This leads to physical destruction and loss of lives or change of form again. That's what it's all about, constant change, with all the earthquakes, tidal waves, cyclones etc. It's only change and we all will be better off in the end. With change comes renewal and with renewal comes new opportunities.

Remember when I went through the change and my lung capacity increased by 30%, I breathe and smell like a person of an age long past. Think of the other species of humans; why did they disappear and not us? Was it because we were stronger or smarter? No, it's because we were able to adapt to the change in a climate with lessening oxygen and other essentials elements in the air that declined. So to evolve to a higher level we, and the rest of the species on earth, must have the proper elements in the air we breathe to survive and thrive and to be more prosperous.

Also remember that the size of the mammals and species has declined through the ages; each has gotten smaller with less oxygen to breathe. Look at us today. Many are wheezing their way through life, not even considering asthma and other diseases in small children.

The lack of oxygen produces the inability to get oxygen to the blood and help the immune system to function correctly. The trees lack carbon dioxide to breath. They produce the oxygen and the process declines slowly over hundreds and thousands of years. Rebuilding the carbon dioxide in the atmosphere is one of the most important steps to help the planet to thrive. All species are dying because of the lack of oxygen (and it takes carbon dioxide to create oxygen).

# 11 Who AM I?

Here is a little more about me before I continue with the Journey. As I said, I am a regular guy who one year ago would never have contemplated writing more than a paragraph as a note to a client.

I haven't written anything of any significance since high school English class. When I went through the change I thought, "This is awesome. I feel good and now I can do a little more than I have in the past." As I had told you, as I approached my 45th birthday I was wondering how much longer I could do what I do. I'd been doing my quite physical work for nearly 25 years and it was taking a toll. I thought, "Oh I can do this another 10 maybe 15 years tops." But almost a year later I feel good, I have none of the physical maladies that I had before and my brain is clear. I wake up and I am alert within five minutes. Before it was two to three hours before I came fully to life. It's a full 360 degree change. I was even what people might call a grump. I never would read a book. Maybe an article in a magazine or paper and even that would be an effort. Now I can skim through a book, grasp the important information in one shot and remember it. Before, a page would take 2.5 minutes or more. Now it's three and four pages in that time and it's still awesome.

By the end of January, I'd been talking to people and I didn't know what I was going to do with all this knowledge. As I talked to people I learned more and more about how to present this knowledge. Each person gave me a new approach, a new angle on it. One person suggested I write a book about my experiences. I said, "It's already been written." But a couple weeks later my spirit spoke to me through my channeling. I auto channel. That is, when a point is very important, my spirit speaks to me.

As I was sleeping it said, "All knowledge is within your grasp!" I didn't even recognize it at that time. I didn't have that much time on my hands. I work 6 days a week, about 65-70 hours, at my business. I'm not some guru sitting on a mat all day eating bread, drinking water and meditating. The average person has a busy life and isn't that easy to find time to write.

So as I'm writing this book the thought is flowing. I ask a question or have a thought about something and the ideas and visions of those thoughts flow. It's like watching a movie. The same thing happens if I'm talking to someone on a particular subject. Everything is just there in my mind's eye and it comes out of me.

In the summer and fall, I listened to the spiritual writers and speakers on the radio, and I also skimmed through a book or two, something I would see on someone's desk or from one of the churches' libraries.

I was listening for someone who was going to tell me they knew this stuff. Some would have a piece or two but no one put it together. I remember a doctor from LA with his book telling me about evolving the mind in the way I have told you to do, but then he went off in another direction with saying 100 people forcing their thought can only move iron fillings a few inches. Another I heard was talking about how we are a division of the whole universe, like I said. But then he couldn't understand what the purpose of everything was, saying that we were here to learn, and if we didn't then there was some price to pay on the other side.

These researchers, and even people who have had experiences similar to mine, are still in the illusion that gets in the way of the full truth as I have laid it out. It is so simple that it seems too good to be true; but it is. They know some of the truth, as I said, but without the full understanding they will not get it. The master said, "The first will be last and the last will be first." Those on the inside, the researchers, cannot see the evidence in front of them. The ones on the outside go with their experience and see it in its simplicity.

Then there are the Religious writers who question the church and their own faith and yet don't understand what God really is. Their nature is telling them to look further and find what the point of everything is. Some believe we are merely a spark of the divine, instead of understanding that the divine is us. I thought I found someone who wrote about it then he went off on Evil, Sin and all the negative garbage that religion talks down to us about.

There's no one or I haven't found anyone yet that really does know.

Take what I say and don't believe in me. Believe in yourself, after all it's all about you; because there is but one!

Look at your world around you, the holy triangle is everywhere. Look at the specifics of every phrase you see, sentence you read: a sign on the street, commercials, a flower, a tree. Spirit told me information like this. Everything is simple, you can figure anything out. You just have to slow it down, break it down. Anything is understandable if you break it down to its essential elements.

You experience knowledge.

Remember I died and was controlled by Spirit for four days. I know it's hard to grasp, even for me. I questioned for a long while, even with the physical changes, but the experience changed me into believing, and understanding came over time.

# 12 How We Can Be

Let's continue the journey now. Through the late fall into November, I purchased the complete set of *Conversations with God* books, 1, 2 and 3. I now consider these books a reference guide to all the principals and laws, some of which are given to us in the holy books by the masters but not explained. I had only read Book 1 by October. In November I read and retained the two other books in the series, a total of 700 plus pages, in 4 weeks of only a couple hours here and there.

Around Christmas I talked to people with the theme of Christmas is not Christ's birth date but an example of our true nature; goodness, fairness and truth or love. And people were very responsive at that time. That led to January when I discovered that I could change my way of bringing in energy. In the big church I saw a picture of Jesus with his hands out by his sides, his thumb and forefinger slightly curled and the rest curled up. I tried it and it was like a direct current. The first time it was totally awesome. The next time I did it, it started slowly and got stronger until I almost blew a circuit by doing it.

That brings up another point. I experience very good feelings all the time. Everything I do feels good or great. Pain is almost non-existent. I can bump my knee, elbow or foot, turn an ankle or stub my toe without feeling pain.

Sometimes it does happen and can be very intense; but by thought control I can block it out.

Remember every state of being is a state of mind. We do that in the same way as a prayer, know that we have received it in gratitude with no doubt. I have said this to introduce the subject of addictions. Everyone wants to feel the high energy of the oneness that we experienced as a small child. That's why we drink alcohol, take drugs, have an addiction to sex, gamble or indulge in any other addictions. This is eliminated because you feel good all the time. This feeling does ebb and flow like everything, but the unnatural highs and lows are not there so the addiction is gone. There is no need to seek an unnatural or induced high.

The last week of January I found my mission or my reason for being. It was just being, and understanding that my place is to lift hearts and to explain with understanding. With each person I use a different approach as the opportunities and choices comes in.

I made a prayer that week for giving Vancouver the best weather possible to show Vancouver and British Columbia in the best light during the Olympics. I know that the weather in Vancouver in February can be very rainy, cloudy and miserable. For the most part during the games the weather was very good. You can come up with any number of excuses to explain the weather, but if you understand why I did that prayer then you know. It was all about fire, light, flame. Light elevates hearts, and that was the goal! It wasn't about sport. Amateur sport is meant to be different from professional but sometimes it's almost the same. In this case it was about showing Canada and the world how all people can get along, in harmony, brotherhood/sisterhood and love. The way the world could be. Did you notice that the security people had little or nothing to do. Again this is an example of our true nature. We are self regulating beings. We are good, fair and live in truth. This is how the world will be, not a hell in a hand basket, like some believe. When we evolve we act in this way.

Evolved people do not kill, harm or deceive others; they do things in their lives with honesty, integrity and truth. If you repeat it enough you will understand. This is our future.

Some ask, "Why do bad things always happen to people? Does God care like a parent should?" Of course Universal Mind does! We are not getting what we want because we make the choices we do. Remember you are the creator of your thoughts; if something negative happens, change to positive and move forward. Those things do not need to happen again and again. We create those things by thinking negative thoughts. Why don't we make the correct choices for ourselves? Again, because we doubt what choice we really have. We have been programmed to believe there is no choice, we must live with what we get and what just comes to us. Why?

Remember at the beginning when I died and Spirit revived me it said, "Do not heed the false prophets!" Who and what are the false prophets? Did the master not warn us of listening to the false doctrine? What is the false doctrine?

1. Teaching the principal of separation, that we are separate from God and each other. This enables us to treat one another as we do; allowing killing, starvation and lack of equality in the world, which allows those in power to profit and control from this separation.

2. That our true nature is evil or bad, that we are evil or truly bad by nature and that we cannot be trusted to run our lives without some type of overseers or government, that killing or some security force is the only way to overcome this flaw in our nature and that we will never be able to live in harmony with each other.

3. That we own something; that anyone owns an individual anything, husband, wife, child, pet or land; that it belongs to an individual or group; that we can give up land when we do not own that we have the right to treat anyone or anything as if we own it.

This false doctrine was created by those who wish to control everything and to profit by that control; making us feel less than what we are, what the masters taught us, twisting and changing their words to that end.

This false doctrine has created the world we live in. The lack of sense of being in all makes us unable to answer this question about why these things happen. If we took back control in our life then these questions would be eliminated, because we would make the choices we want, create our own desires and make them happen.

Remember everything is about trust or faith. That is the whole point in this book, trust yourself. Look at it this way:

- with no faith you will probably drown in the sea of doubt;
- with blind faith you will keep your head above water in the sea of doubt;
- absolute faith is certainty with purpose. That purpose will create your life and you will lack nothing.

## 13 Certainty of Being

Let me tell you the last example before I get to the solutions I promised you. The morning of February 28, 2010, at about 1:00 am I prayed, "Thank you for allowing Canada to win the gold medal hockey game, so it may lift the hearts of all Canadians." I got home at 6:00 am and had the month end paperwork to do. I didn't get done until about 8:00 am and then went to bed. I couldn't sleep much because Spirit started telling me things that I needed know about this book. I heard my wife cheering as she watched the gold medal hockey game. I got up during the third period. I had told her Canada would win and I wasn't worried even when the game was tied and went into overtime. I said no doubt, no doubt, no doubt in the overtime. Three seconds later Canada scored and won. I had told my wife at the end of regular time that this would just make it more interesting with no worries at all. I feel a game now, I can listen or watch the start of any game and feel the energy level of the players and know what the probable result will be, as long as I tune in. Professional sport is all about winning. It's a simulated warfare, and that's what the powers that be want. We are to be at a constant state of readiness and keep our minds on the separation of everyone. Winning and losing is not our natural state; equality in all things is

our state. Entertainment should not be about winning or
losing. Sport was invented as a bonding experience with
games of throwing and running at the community
gatherings as friendly competition. It wasn't supposed to
be about warfare. Professional sport's only redeeming
quality is for the fans, the ability to bond and feel a sense
of community. International competition is different
though. For everyone, both players and fans, it's for
country and community.

Some people say coincidences happen but most know
that coincidences never happen. Why is that? Does the
holy book not say that there is nothing new under the
sun? What does that mean? Does it not also say that God
is the same today, tomorrow and yesterday? What does
that mean? It means the same thing. Time does not exist,
and everything that has happened and will happen is
happening now. But the future is always changing. That
again is the eternal moment of now. That's why there are
no coincidences. We are that being that lives in all times.
So what am I saying? We are living all these lives at once.
That is why we dream. Dreams are a glimpse of our other
lives. Time is a human construct. We believe time exists,
but it does not.

How that works is that time is not what we think. It's
not a line, it's a spiral, like a vertical coil. This coil
connects to come full circle. Each level of the spiral has a
thin layer or plain of existence. This is where the illusions
come from, those on the plains. They are not good or bad
realms, only other lives. All is good. We live on these
plains, constantly moving from plain to plain in the one

life that we live. This is why our body is stiff and paralysed when we sleep. That's why sleep is so important to the body and spirit.

That is why nothing matters—no thing matters. Everything has already happened, and we are living it. That's why nothing is a coincidence. We are just experiencing and feeling it, emotion in motion. Remember when I spiralled back from the light to my body on May 4th, 2009, this was the spiral of the plains of existence. We live on those plains when we sleep. A day in that existence or this one could be a few seconds of our sleep time in this body. As we sleep we spin through these lives one level at a time, spinning up and down in a circle. As I just said, your dreams are but a glimpse of this.

Does your life serve you in the way you want? If so it's your path. If not then change it, it's your choice. We are here to serve ourselves by serving others. No one's path can be changed by us except our own. That's why nothing matters as well. It is difficult to understand all the good, bad or indifferent behaviour and be able to cope or not judge. In the end, it is what it is. It doesn't matter. I had a hard time with this one, too. If we understand that everything is, was and will be, then it's easy to understand. Serve your path and help others serve theirs. No judgments, just do it, go with the flow. It's just a part of the process and we are the process. Always remember what we are and it will be easier and easier. Sometimes I still second guess it when I see apparent injustice happening but that's the divine dichotomy. It always shows up. We are and we are not; always and forever. We cannot not be.

So let's do a quick review of the basics before I go to some possible processes to change our path to more enlightenment. We are a division of the whole of the All of Everything, the everlasting source of the entire universe, the process of it all. We have a veil of misunderstanding put on us at a young age so we can forget and then later remember. Then we are programmed to become what we are not, the opposite of who we are.

The three laws are:
- Thought is energy
- Fear attracts like energy
- Love is all there is; our fullness

We live this life and other lives as an experience, no two experiences are ever the same. The main principles are:
- Do not worry and number one love your neighbour as yourself;
- We are one with everything/what we hold (worry about) we push away, what we give away we receive back 10, 20, 30 fold. It's better to give than receive. Don't expect a payoff.
- Everyone or thing has their own path, everything has a spirit, each spins at their own rate, speed of thought
- Everything is a thinking thing,
- The Holy Triangle is the All of Everything; everything is a three-part being.

- We create by thought—word—action with gratitude and no doubts as if we have already received in our supplemental or sponsoring thought. It is very important that it believes. Say it three times to focus the thought. Be specific in that focused thought.
- We can reprogram our brain by changing our thoughts with conceive—create—experience and thereby evolving our brain.
- Change your state of being by changing your mind. Mass consciousness is very powerful, especially when it is focused on worry. It can override a single person's focused thought over time because it does it unconsciously. Study the myths, legends and holy books for examples of all the principles and laws that are hidden; we need to teach them with positive understanding to help awaken people.

Remember the scientists have figured out the what of the universe but not the how or the why. Energy is the All of Everything in the physical universe. Scientists have found energy tornados inside atoms. We will never end. We are the process, we are the mind and spirit, the universe (form) is the body. Remember everything is the Holy Triangle. The master said, "For those who have eyes to see and ears to hear." It's everywhere all around us. Be specific, not general, and you will see it. All is divine! Remember there is no good or bad, evil, sin or karma. They are all part of the illusion. Everything is opportunity and choice.

# 14 Where Are We Going?

Before I start of the process of presenting the solutions, let's observe the world we live in today. If you choose to change something, you should know what it is that needs to be changed. Also, who or what makes this current system run? Is it we, the whole of the people, or is it a small group of people? It's 1% that runs this world. I am saying all this as an observation! Does this world serve you? If not then here's what it is. I've always said this, this is nothing new to me. You may have differing observations. We live in a modem day feudal system. What's the feudal system? That is the system that ran most of the world and even today runs things.

As you may remember from you school studies, the feudal system was, as I described in the mechanics paragraph, a system where the kings and the lord of the land ruled over the serfs and others. The serfs worked the land and paid heavy taxes to the landowner for use of the land which they worked and lived on. This system was highly beneficial to the lord, however the serfs could never move ahead, only continually struggle to survive.

Now move ahead 600-1,000 years and ask yourself, "Has it changed very much?" We may have advances in technology but has it changed? We work for a living, pay income taxes, pay for our house, car, furniture, credit cards etc., to whom? The governments, banks, credit card companies or other lending institutions. Who owns them? The same people own them, the descendants of the lords and kings. They didn't lose their land, they sold it and bought large shares of the banks and other corporations from which we buy all our essentials. These banks, governments and corporations run our world and we are in the same roles as always. These corporations make profits on us in the western world and take advantage of the other 70% of the world's population to draw their resources and labour, and use their space to dump hazardous materials.

When we live in honesty, integrity and truth we do not profit to the detriment of others. We run our personal, business and corporate lives in truth and everyone benefits. Some say that we will work out a political solution but who do the politicians serve? They don't serve us, they serve the 1%. The status quo is more profitable to them. Remember how they programmed our brain through minimize, marginalize and mechanize? They were the ones doing it to us. Their grip is loosening the last couple decades. Tools like the internet also work both ways. They help some people clearly identify the illusion while others become more deeply entrenched. We see the young people today who have become like machines. When they are unplugged from the internet, they cannot function as an individual person. They have become part of the machine. I see very few young people protesting the system like other generations have.

This is what we are here for, to be individuals and think for ourselves. We come from the collective mind, yet each experience is meant to be different. When we cannot do that we are lost. The only time the collective mind is a good thing is when we work together to build something, and then become an individual again. That is not happening with our youth. That's why they seem or are like machines. I see the youthful people walking and their feet are dragging along the ground. Youth should glide or float across the ground. I watch people more now than I ever have and I see younger and younger people like that. This is not to say that a computer is not a great tool, but use it as a tool, not a total connection with everything. It will disable your mind, stop you from thinking for yourself.

As I was saying, we are and will get loose from this grip when we change our thinking. Does this world serve you? If so then be happy with it However, I see so many people who are unhappy, stuck to the ground, their eyes are downcast and lost in the struggle to cope. These are things I was as well. These things are signs of the programming we are a product of, the fear that is constantly imposed on us. Why? For the reasons I've just given to you.

Some believe in the mythology of a religious saviour or some other mythological being coming to save the "good people" and destroy the "bad people" and that this is the end of the world. Universal Mind said it is the beginning and the end with NO END. Remember the circle of life, the physical experience, has no end. Some believe that a light or an alignment of the planets in 2012 will have a spiritual awakening happen.

These are myths as well. The way we will evolve is by one person changing, acting and showing the example to others, and then one by one other people will change. Doing what works. Other planets do things like this. On our planet we only do what works for the elite.

By doing it first in our home, workplace and the community we become a leader of people, an example, a shining light. Others will follow and spread the word. Change will happen and we will evolve to what we choose to be, not what we are told to be. This is the process to follow:

1. Teach this knowledge: Teach the positive messages that have been given us by our masters, our teachers. Throw out the negative mythologies and stop the fear programming at every turn. The churches of all the religions are dying or are in the total control of the government with their negative programming. No peace is to be had by any of them. All people seek peace, harmony and fairness. Teach these messages of positivity, hope and truth, and they will be blessed even further. What you bind on Earth, hold onto or worry about, you bind in heaven; the truth. What treasure you give away on Earth will be yours in heaven; that is love. What you give away you receive back 10, 20, 30 fold. If these things are followed then the spiritual awakening will occur, and no one will be denied the truth because once our brain is clear the truth comes to us. As I said earlier, Spirit wants to contact us through pure thought,

pure emotion and pure experience, and the experience will change us to what we are.

2. Become aware of the killing and security machine This machine is sponsored by the profit making process that only thinks of profit; not the results. We are self regulating beings. Governments want to control and through our programming we gives them authority. We can manage ourselves with government as an administrative body only. Government and education structures will change to accommodate these changes. The trillions of dollars used in this security system will be funnelled to a central structure to help bring equity to all, not power to the very few who profit from the current system. We will refocus technology and use it in other areas.

3. Return to traditional medicines and healing practices: healing medicines, foods, herbal remedies and healing practitioners. Retrain doctors to use these products and to return to the two snakes of the medical sciences: medicine, spiritual healing and setting of bones. Socrates himself said in the future patients will heal themselves. There will be self healing as well through spiritual training as I did. The drug companies can return to their original purpose, producing plant based medicines, by adjusting their focus and growing herbal remedies. Chemical based drugs are only masking, addicting and killing people; not healing. Not all drugs and surgeries will be gone. There are some very necessary practices. The trillions spent by governments

on drugs can also be funnelled to a central structure to help bring equality to all.

These things can be done in a short period of time depending on what the masses want and if they are awakened by the teachings. It may take 10 years or 100 or 500, but it does not matter for we are always evolving to this new world. Look at it this way, the money saved by taking steps 2 and 3 will lift billions out of poverty. Look what happened in China when 300 million were lifted from poverty, the economy of the world benefited greatly. Imagine 2, 3, 4 billion lifted up. The high tide lifts all boats. When these things are done the world will be ready and willing to move to a new golden age. Remember the dream of Nebakadnezar, the king of Persia? Daniel translated his dream of the statue of golden head, silver neck, bronze shoulder, iron torso and legs and clay feet.

We are currently at the end of the Iron Age. This will be followed by the age of clay, which is the age of transition and which we may be entering very soon. This age is a return to core values and fundamental techniques. Then we will emerge to a new golden age that will last as long as we choose it to, not making the mistakes of the past because we have the whole truth and nothing but the truth!

When you understand all that we are, you will feel as I do. True freedom and total complete joy. A joy that no one or thing can take from us no matter the circumstances. My sole purpose for this book is to tell the truth. Some will love me, then hate me. Some will want me dead because it goes against everything that they believe. But after they kill me they will love me again. This freedom and joy has no rival in my life. I feel totally incredible with this thought. It is total trust in who I am, the process of what I am, and I will continue with the process.

This transitional age will bring us back old knowledge to cleanse our spirit and old, but new knowledge to move forward with.

There are those who still say, "But the Earth cannot take the whole world in an equal economy." They haven't been listening.

Thought—word—action or deed never fails for each region to supply this warehouse Earth with everything that is needed: water, food, resources, rain where needed and any other weather or other requirement to supply all our needs. The size of the population won't matter because we will live in plenty, not lack as we have for thousands of years. Lack is profitable for the few. Plenty is profit for all.

Learn who we are, know it and use it with purpose. These things will come to pass eventually, and it is already happening. We are always revolving— evolving—spinning forward. That is our nature.

That is love in motion. What kind of a world do you wish to live in, a world of hardship—heartlessness— hatred or a world of hope—heart—happiness? We, the majority, always prefer the latter. All are one and one for all live in peace, hope and love. That is creating instant evolution—love in motion! And with that I hope that the people of earth will allow themselves to let the grief of death and disaster slide away and see the truth, that it is only change of form, and that no thing ever dies. Joy peace and love go with you all the days of your life. Allow this writing to give you the total freedom that we all seek.

# Book 2
# Creating Instant Joy
# Love the Experience

# Introduction

I am writing this book six months after I finished *Creating Instant Evolution, Love in Motion*, which I will refer to in this book as Book 1. That book was the Journey of my Instant evolution, my process of the Learning and Practice of the laws and principals that govern the universe. This book is about the emotion of the Journey and the changes I've gone through since writing Book 1. It's about helping you create the joy in your life or experience by understanding who we are, what we are and the process which we are in. I'll also delve a little deeper into the explanation of the system that works against us all in finding our true nature and that prevents us from enjoying our experience. I'll refer back to Book 1 throughout this book. As those who have read it know, I approach this topic with full knowing and understanding because of my Death, Revival and being fully aware for nearly four days back in May of 2009. I know of what I speak. I'll give you more examples of my growing understanding along with a review of some of the basics. I want to help you to understand and, with understanding, gain certainty, purpose and passion for this life. Those are the goals of this writing.

# 1 Who, What We Are

I'll do a quick review of who we are, what we are and the process which we are in.

We are a three part being or a Triune. Everything in the physical universe is a three part being. That is why the scientists cannot figure it out. They only focus on the what, not the how or the why. We are Body (Universe/Physical), Mind (Universal mind) All That Is, "It" which is, the oneness of All or God/Goddess) and Spirit (A division of the whole, the expression of the one and or love or the experience of All that is). We are the body or an avatar for our thought (Universal Mind) and consciousness (Spirit). We are God made manifest to put it in the simplest terms. That is who and what we are. The process we are in is very simple, as I just said above. We are the experience of All That Is. So we are here to simply experience our lives. That is our only purpose. Through my experience on May 6th 2009, I have total knowing of this. I was dying on the living room floor in my house and I asked for help that I knew would come. Because I had been warned two days earlier that I may lose the ones I loved, I was lying face down on that mat and thinking that I was not going to go like Heath Ledger had a few weeks earlier, naked on the floor. When I asked for help, the force of a freight train came through me, blowing the drug out of my body, pushing me to the complete and total limitation of my body. The other things are documented in Book 1. Spirit carried me for nearly four days. The power that I had was so awesome I didn't know how to feel, but it was very good. This is coming from a guy who was always considered the weakling. I was never confident like that and the strength was intoxicating and a rush, even after the clearing and my adjustment to my new body. The power is still there, especially when I need it. It feels great when my head and my cheeks get hot (that's when the energy, from Universal Mind and Spirit, is high) It's always there and it modifies itself (remember thought is energy). This is how I know this. I speak truth, and I live in this joy of knowing, total knowing.

To continue on what the process is, if you understand that we are the experience of All That Is, then we are an unlimited being that lives with no beginning or end. No matter what happens in this life, or others that we live, there is no end to this process.

We also live hundreds of lives at the same time. That is what our dream life is; it's a remembrance of the lives that we live while the body (this body on this plain) sleeps. Our spirit leaves our body whenever we sleep, be it a few seconds or hours. We feel the bliss when we are falling off to sleep—that is us leaving our body—and the start we feel is us reentering the body. Once you understand this process then you understand that nothing matters—death, misery or other things—because we are that we are and the life we lead here on this plain is only one of many. The most important part of this understanding is that we are the Created and the Creator, a sum of the parts of All That Is. How do we create? As I said in Book 1, thought (conceive the thought in the mind), word (speak the thought in specifics with total gratitude as if you've already received and no doubt in the supplemental thought, that is the sponsoring thought behind the thought) and action or deed (the manifestation of the action or deed by Universal Mind). This is the process of creation and, in trusting in it, you create your life with certainty, purpose and the passion for life.

## 2 Show Me Trust

As I had told those who read Book1, the power, the love and the trust were shown to me during the four day period that I was fully in Spirit. I will go a little deeper to show you the trust. This has continued to grow stronger and I trust even more now. It is hard going backwards. Living in the now, the eternal moment of now, is a very light, positive energy. Going back or forward creates negative energy that can make us heavy or give us headaches or stress on the body. This is why we stay in the now. The day I died and was brought back by Spirit was a Wednesday, and a lot of things happen on Wednesdays. That day the power that came through me was awesome. I had never thought this was possible because I had lived in fear my entire life. I really didn't know it at the time but I felt the entire weight of the world on me and had no confidence. This event totally changed my outlook from that second. No matter what happened in the sequences of events, the confidence in Spirit was totally overwhelming. I knew it was my true identity instantly. I went from the shy guy with no confidence to writing this book! Yes, because I want everyone in the world to be free if they choose! I've always rallied against the system and that's why I called the pastors to give them a scare and shake them up a bit.

I encountered them on a few occasions and Spirit gave them a piece of its mind. I'd never have done that in the past. I was the shy humble guy who works in a profession that doesn't get enough respect anywhere in the world. I've always worked by will, determination and mental effort, because my body was weighed down with heaviness. Until a few months ago, I didn't realize what that was. I knew there was a weight but I didn't know it was emotional weight. A lot of people experience this in their lives and, like me, do not realize what it is.

I didn't trust anyone from childhood. The details aren't important, just that it's a state that a lot of people can relate to. Even my family life didn't give me the trust that I should have had. Then I went to the light and was brought back by Spirit. It told me one of the primary things was "trust". Since then I've learned to trust everything. It wasn't easy at first. I was trying to deal with the events of that week in May and then adjusting to my new body and understanding all that I am. This took a few months and, as I learned the principals, I looked at my past and analyzed my life through those principals. And trust came. All through the events of May 9th 2009, I was totally in spirit. When I said to my wife, "I made love to you," the feeling inside of me was that of total, complete peace and love, like nothing I've ever felt before. And also when I told my sister that I loved her in spirit the same feeling arose in me. This feeling, as I said, is the only feeling that we are. And we want to feel this always!

Once I came to this understanding with help from my mom and the information in *Conversations With God* books by Neale Donald Walsh, I started to totally trust, especially after I learned how to manifest or ask to manifest things and they occurred. Trust that all is available at your asking. Always the key to universal love is TRUST!

# 3 Heaviness Is Gone!

The Monday after I did the "clearing" (May 9th) I went to the healer again and had a session, the last one I needed. I went home and had a nap before I had to go to work. When I was about to go to sleep, I followed an exercise that the healer had given me to do; it was like when you are coming down from altitude and clearing you head. Except this was my entire body unplugging, and I felt the energy flowing out of all my extremities— all of them: hands, feet and even penis. It was incredible. After all the stiffness in my body was gone, the lightness in my fingers, feet, elbows, shoulders, everything was great. I could feel the floor with my feet. I couldn't remember any time in my life when I could feel the floor.

The next day, I stopped at a supplier to pick up a few things. The owner was there and I started talking to her about the change. She had read all the books by Neale Donald Walsh. But she had no physical connection to what I had experienced. I told her, "I feel so light, I've never felt like this ever. It used to always be an effort even to walk, every step required a thought." She said I looked totally different and went on about how her brother was totally sold on the ideas but had no physical changes. My mom told me there are a lot of people who are informed but do not really understand. This is why

I'm writing these books so others may get a better sense of how it is.

As I had told you in the last chapter, before the event everything was will, determination and mental effort. Now I just do it, go with the flow. It was a physical relief to just go, no mental effort required to do anything. The heaviness was gone, in all areas. I felt odd and I continued to follow my same habits but the lightness didn't leave me.

Even though I was following those habits which were against the flow (listening to negative stuff on the radio and TV, allowing negative things to enter my brain), I was learning, especially through those first two months. My mom helped a lot with her advice and listening to my progress. My mind was way ahead of my body at this point. The thought energy was very high and it carried my body. (Example of my playing golf and losing it at the end of a round). By October my body had recovered enough to start rebuilding, but it still wasn't totally recovered until the middle of winter.

I recall listening to that late night radio show probably in late May. A man named Dr. Bruce Pearl (I believe) was on and he said, "All I say every morning is 'Thank You!'" I now do the same. I previously did say a prayer of thanksgiving every morning, thanking Father/Mother for helping out all those in need, for family and for all my blessings, health, etc.

He (Dr. Pearl) related the story of three angels hiding human's true identities. The first one said, "Let's hide it on top of the highest mountain."

The others said, "They will find it there."

The next one said, "Let's hide it at the bottom of the deepest ocean."

The others said, "They will find it there."

The last one said, "Let's hide it inside of the humans. They will never find it there."

This is where I discovered the energy transmitter in my brain, as I've told you before. I said, "I am a light and energy being," three times and the energy went out of the top of my head. This transmission is very strong. Whenever I say a prayer, the energy builds as I say the prayer and after I say it for the third time, the prayer (thought energy) releases out of the top of my head and I am forced to make an Awh! noise. It varies depending on the strength of the energy. (The only way I can describe it is that it's like when you have a climax during sex, although not quite as intense) The energy was still very strong in my body and the energy going out was a real rush. Remember this is how we communicate with the Universal Mind.

During those first couple months, I hadn't yet touched a book on the subject. I felt strong and I felt weak. Sometimes I had to take a power nap two or three times a night (while at work). My body just couldn't keep up yet. I felt awesome after two to five minutes of sleep and could go for another three to four hours. Then I would crash again. The lightness, the strength and the feeling of the energy was always there.

I recall listening one night (on the same radio show) to a scientist who was talking about the formation of the universe and talking about the big bang. I saw in my third eye (Mind's eye), before he even mentioned it and before I had read any books about our true divine nature, what the actual event looked like. I used my experiences as a guide.

Those first few months were tough because I was fighting the reality of what I am as opposed to what the world tells me I am. It was a constant battle. Am I right or is the world right? Even after I started reading *Conversation with God*, my experience with the words of the Bible and other worldly experiences always brought me to the same conclusions—I am that I am. Everything that happens to me and was happening was real and true.

I went from knowing to not knowing, and that's the divine dilemma. It comes and goes until we fully understand what we are. I talked to a few people to get my story right and to assure myself that I wasn't off my rocker. I knew I wasn't and the logical mind couldn't convince me, although it surely tried. This battle is always won by the heart and our pure emotion and experiences. My mom told me at the beginning of all this that it was a lonely road because not many truly understand what we are. She was a great support and is still there to share my experiences.

Remember I mentioned at the beginning of the second chapter about heavy and light energy. Heavy energy is produced by worrying about the past or future. The past is done and the future is always changing so live in the now. It is light, and we flow through the light. Therefore the heaviness that I felt was the negative energy produced by looking backwards or forwards and not going with the flow. Think of the light energy as love energy allowing you to be the fullness of who you are; all the confidence, trust and faithfulness. Light energy also lets you experience the strength, power and mental capacity that you've always had. The heaviness was the lack of love, trust and confidence weighing me down. This heavy energy weighs many of us down because we do not know or believe in the universal truth of love. One quick example of this is that when I allow the worldly problems to enter my mind, I can feel a small amount of heaviness, but when I remember the light, it slips away. Dark (heavy energy) cannot stand in the light. Always remember this.

## 4 Love You So

The Tuesday in May after my clearing was the 12th. I was talking on the phone to Rachel, who was one year old at the time. She could only cry and make noises. I was still really high on spirit energy. She was crying and I distinctly heard her say, "Love you so." This is the love of all that we are. The child knows the truth and she was supporting me through my change. This is the same voice that she now uses at two-and-a-half years old, same tone, everything. Think again of the small child as the prime example to follow. The love that I feel from this love energy is pure and gives me the best high that one could attain, but it is totally controllable. That is, when we attain this level, it's under our control.

This energy I call the love drug, connects us directly to spirit and mind. One's head and cheeks become very hot. This connection reinforces the total peace and love that we feel and makes us know all that we are. I can bring this in and be very high, strong and focused in a matter of less than thirty seconds, and I can increase it until it makes my head and body tingle. I feel the force field between my hands no matter how far apart they are. I don't need to ever bring my hands together. All I need to do is have a positive thought and it flows in my fingers. I explained in Book 1 about the positioning of my fingers.

This love, that connects me to the universe, allows me to know that this connection is with all, everything being one thing. I give respect to all. Sometimes in the beginning if I hurt something, like stepping on a spider, I'd say, "Sorry." Now I am more conscious about avoiding hurting, always speaking to everything as if to a friend. I know that I am one with them and I or you never know if that other person may be us in another life. That's the cosmic wheel. We start at one point (slowest to fastest spinning thought energy) and work our way around it. It's our choice as always.

Think of this love energy as a bubble around us. It envelopes us, surrounds us with love, that which we are. This bubble of love is what, when I am going really fast, pushes things around, makes them fly off the shelf. Or if I bump into something, I bounce off with no pain. Think of the entire physical universe as this bubble of love, a safe, secure playground for us to play in. We, mind and spirit, are playing the game called life. Think of it as your personal movie where you are the lead actor, director and screenwriter. All the others are only bit players and you are a bit player in their movie. All these players interact to form the total, complete matrix of the big movie called life. But remember you are always in control if you know this, you trust love and have faithfulness to All That Is.

This matrix of people, things and beings works the same way as the matrix of energy for we are the thought energy manifest that runs the universe. The interaction and the interdependence is so magnificent that we overlook it because we can't see past our own life. We feel unimportant in the grand scheme of things but our experience is as important as everyone and everything in the universe. When you feel the love of the whole you will see that you are the most important person, being or thing that is. This love lifts us, holds us and sustains us through everything we encounter. This love makes one on one love seem small in comparison. Not that it is unimportant as it is all we are. This love makes us want more of life, not just the small things. It makes us want to share this love with all. It makes us want to embrace all that life has to offer and more, much more. Sharing this love is what we want to be at our core. I can no longer **feel** a person approaching me like I used to—some call it radar—I just **know** they are there and I turn and there they are. We are one energy in this love bubble. When you know it, it just is. I don't question it because I know it now.

These writings are on purpose, and I write them with certainty. They aren't someone musing on a theoretical point. I know this and feel it every day. My entire being and state of being has changed since I wrote Book 1. I am physically, mentally and emotionally there. I'm not growing into it like a lot of others. In the past I had been comfortable with everything that had happened but my connection came and went. With the writing of that book, this bond has increased probably thirty fold. I feel my total fullness of love, peace and connection with everything. I have found the middle way, or even keel, not too much in the spirit and not completely in the physical.

On August 14, 2010, I got a tattoo put on my left forearm. It's a circle with three flares of the sun (to indicate a spinning action) and the colours of the rainbow bleeding into the centre which is LOVE. On the outside it says ALL IS. ALL IS LOVE. It was supposed to take an hour and a half to put it on but I was talking to the tattoo artist and it took only half the time. And I didn't feel much pain at all. The artists and patrons in the shop were pretty amazed that it took only half that time. They listened to my story and were all smiles after we were done. This tattoo was suggested by Spirit as a teaching tool and a constant reminder to me of what and who I am. It has worked pretty well so far as a teaching tool. One person in a store asked me about it. I told her what it meant and it confirmed her beliefs. I got a thank you and a smile from her. Later I had a very good feeling of almost bliss come over me. It carried me for several hours that night. When we share, it brings out the best from our core.

As I am writing this the thought energy is flowing and my cheeks are on fire. It reminds me of the Talking Heads song "Burning Down the house".

I'll go back now to the weeks following the clearing and discuss the adjustments to the new power, strength and ability with my left side. It was great in one regard but my body felt physical stress as I said earlier when I mentioned the napping. It felt sometimes like a rope was around my chest. I had a tendency to roar a lot, I can feel the power in the roars, a HUH, HUH! noise I make. It was strength from the core of my being to overcome the physical stress. The thought was strong, like I said earlier, but the body wasn't ready to be used to total capacity as it is today. I started writing this in late September 2010.

The first two weeks I ran on salads, fruit and water my thought energy was strong. I went from 175 pounds to 156 pounds. I don't recommend this as a diet unless you have a lot of really strong mental toughness to overcome the urge for more substantial foods. By the third week of May, I was balanced, and I had adjusted my pressure on the strength and power side as well. I would just go, go, go because I felt so good mentally. That has not changed very much. I do want to just be at times now.

This love energy was flowing through me, ebbing and flowing with no real control at that point. Sometimes, when I was working, my feet would burn for a few seconds as the energy left my body. As I said before, I hardly feel pain. That coming from a guy who would wince in pain before I would even hit anything. Or the thought of hitting something would cause me to say Ahh!

This bubble of love around me took a time of adjustment as well. I'd hit a corner of something and I'd say, "Ahh." But then I'd say, "What did you say that for? It didn't hurt." I got to the point where I'd slam a body part into a wall or bounce off a wall to prove to myself that it didn't hurt. After a while it was a lost cause to even think about it. Sometimes, to prove a point, I'd slam my elbow really hard on a counter top. It hurt a little but the person I was with would say, "I can't do that!" This bubble is what makes me glide through my day without much effort physically or mentally. I never get tired. Only when I relax my mind do I shut off. There is no mental tiredness that I can recall in the last year or so. I can allow my thoughts to focus on what I'm doing but mostly just let them flow and whatever comes in comes in. This is where the joy begins.

One additional thing since we are talking about emotion here, I was looking for publishers in the library the other week and I found a book on colours and how your favourite colour is related to your spirituality. Mine is orange, so I looked it up and it talked about it as being connected to your solar plexus chakra which is about intuition and emotion. This is where we come in, our belly button that is. Remember I told you in Book 1 that when I went into the light it was orange. At first this was my illusion telling me that this was truth and to follow my emotional intuition. And when I spun back to my body I entered by my solar plexus. This was to tell me it was not a dream. Funny thing that this has always been my favourite colour. Remember love is the highest of our emotions, it is all there is.

# 5 1, 2, 3, To Infinity

In recent days here in early October I have been contemplating how to explain our complete nature to help those who think things were a little too complex to actually be that simple. Especially since we live in a world where complexity is the name of the game. I was talking to my teacher (mother) and came up with a simple way to explain infinity. I started 1, 2, 3, all we are is a three part being and everything is three. Okay so 1 + 1+ 1 is everything. All numbers after three are a multiple of those three. Now all things are a division of the one, All That Is. So I stated one is one and can never be less than. This is again All That Is; source. Two is spirit; thought (mind) and consciousness (spirit). It divided itself into experience and we are the experience or expression of All That Is, the sum of its parts. Divide two by itself and what do you get? Keep dividing the answer by 2 twenty-six times to get zero or one with twenty-five zeros, which is a ten trillion, trillion. Then take three which is the body of the universe (the physical body, mind, spirit) and divide it the same way and you get one with fifteen zeros behind it. This means one with fifteen zeros makes up the physical. But then I said, "How can that be? Twenty-five doesn't go into fifteen." Then we start to understand the real nature of infinity. Remember each spirit has hundreds and hundreds, perhaps thousands, of lives on different plains of existence. Now multiply the twenty-five zero number by many hundreds. Then there are ten billion or one with ten zeros plains of existence. Then you really start to understand (15+10=25) why nothing matters and to live in the now. Because when I hit onto these thoughts, I started to see what the All of Everything truly was. When I finished that, I went in the other direction, from the bigness to the smallness of it all, and my mind started to expand even further. But I had to stop. Because when you get there, the total complete understanding of what we truly are kicks in. It's like hitting the mother lode of knowledge, and I had to stop. My head was hurting and the thought I had a few years ago, that Spirit had given me, came back to me; the universe is bigger than you can image and smaller. I also remember some advice I received right after my clearing and total awakening. Don't allow too much knowledge to come in, it may overwhelm you. I hope I didn't overwhelm you. Some of this stuff is so simple. It's just flowing into my mind and when you combine it with the other knowledge it becomes very deep, too deep for some.

The reason I started down this path to start with was to explain it to the scientific minds that are very hard to crack.

One Labour Day weekend I played golf with a doctor, a brain surgeon. I told him of all my physical changes and talked to him about my return by Spirit. At the end of the day, I was sitting in my truck. He was right beside me getting into his vehicle. He said, "Another guy who thinks he had a near death experience." That pissed me off for a couple of minutes but as always Spirit reminded me that it doesn't matter what others think. Another experience was with a student. I talked with him about the nature of the universe. I told him my story, but I made a couple of numerical errors because I hadn't figured out the numbers yet. He understood but he talked about the string theory that was based on there being only one source of thought energy. As I just explained, there is that of source, or Universal Mind, and ten trillion, trillion other thought energies being generated. The whole point of this chapter is what we are, and the energy generated from our thought energies creates the entire universe in its infinite size and space. It's pretty simple and amazing what we are, isn't it?

Science and the scientific minds of these last few centuries have brought us a lot of great discoveries or uncovered the old knowledge. But they have created a world that only believes in the physical or that which can be physically proved and must be confirmed by others. It has shown the physical in what's explainable. But it has taken true mystery and so-called magic away from us. It has created a world of doubters, a world of people who need to be shown that it's not a lie by proving it in a laboratory or testing it in some way. This is one of the three ways that we have had our joy of life not taken but diminished by doubt, by questioning, removing all the belief in ourselves. This system works its way into all facets of our lives showing us all the what of things and disproving the divine in everything because it is unmeasurable. This is the beginning of the fear factor that we all live under. It permeates our psyche.

But by showing these numbers, we can undermine that programming and help those who choose to again see the magic and the awesome nature of all that we are.

I'll give you a couple of examples of how we have brought everything down to a "show me" state. We have a lack of understanding in a lot of areas because of the "show me" state we live in. These are observations I make, without judgements on anything. It's all part of the experience no matter what. Over the last few years I have seen trans-gender people on the TV talking about how they felt like the opposite sex to what they were, male to female, female to male, saying they felt that they were in the wrong body and couldn't get over it. So they changed sex. But when they got a partner they stuck with the opposite gender to their original gender even when they changed the gender of their experience. I say, "So what was the point in having the sex change operation if they are still partnered up with the one who was originally their opposite?" It was because they couldn't accept who they are and that results in a lack of joy in their life up to that point. We all are trans-gendered beings, we go back and forth between our bodies or lives, changing genders on a regular basis. Our childhood is a transitional period to get used to that body. I recall this happening to me as a young boy, relating to girls more, but when the hormones kicked in I changed. Now how does this pertain to what I'm talking about?

In a world of science we discount the divine in everything, and we don't teach people the truth about themselves in regards to our interchangeable nature, therefore destroying a person's ability to enjoy what they had originally chosen to experience in this life. We choose our experiences before we enter a life (as always everything is choice). However, we lack the knowledge of our true nature and that, in this case, we are both sexes constantly changing from plain to plain. In my life I've often dreamt of both female and male experiences. If we taught this simple principal, people's lives would become less complex and stressful, and we could just enjoy them.

In the late spring of 2010, on a TV program, I saw another scientist speaking to a researcher. He talked about the connection we have with the mechanical universe. This may or may not connect for you. He was a Harvard University Quantum scientist and he made this statement, "One hundred years ago, we thought that physical reality was outside of our ability to influence, but now we believe that our brains have something to do with it." After a hundred years quantum scientists still do not understand the connection we have in creating the world around us, because they cannot measure it in a lab. As I stated earlier, if they allowed these scientist to focus on thought energy they might find their answers. But this doesn't quantify in the scientific mind. As I stated in Book 1, the brain is our receiver and transmitter with Universal Mind, therefore creating our world with it.

Scientists will not grasp this until they open their minds more than ever. Once they do they will help us move forward at a pace never seen in this civilization.

# 6 What is Faithfulness?

Now I'll get back to the third part of creating joy.

What is faithfulness? Faith is trust. Faithfulness is openness or faithful communication. I'll tell you that this one is a little harder to attain. I trusted and believed in what I am, and I had the energy flowing in. I had the love and trust. In January 2010, I really began to connect with Spirit. Although I trusted what I was, the communication wasn't quite there yet. As I said in Book 1, Spirit would come in through an auto channel giving me important information to make sure I wasn't slipping, mainly telling me that it does not matter. I would worry that I needed to tell people things, and I'd get upset if I forgot something.

In late January 2010, I started to understand. Then it became my goal and mission to help others become aware of who and what we are and the process we are in. I told you about the prayers. I had mentioned the Olympics in Vancouver, BC, Canada and the goal of showing people our true nature during them. And they came to pass as I said in Book 1.

So during the Olympics I started Book 1 just to document my experiences and help others towards understanding. That was my only goal. During the writing process, or should I say the thought process, I began to communicate more readily with Spirit.

I would ask a question and a thought would enter my mind. I didn't trust yet if it was me or It. I would get a thought and say, "Clarify, clarify." So it slowed down that thought into normal language which I could understand and use. It would give me an example to answer the question, simple things, things I could use to explain easily. Like: we are a life form, we give form life, we not I. We are life; we are the process of life. Simple phrases. Then I started to trust the communication.

When I asked a question then, I started to get full explanations of things in ways all could understand. Then as I went forward with Book 1, I trusted the knowledge and it became visual, like a movie playing in my head. I now don't question as much, but if I need something, or need to know something, it usually just comes to me either way (thought or visual). Being able to have this faithful communication enables me to be fully confident on any subject that I want to deal with. This reconfirms the love and the trust in all that I am. I would occasionally test it out to see if I was still connected and the answer would come in. This is how my faithfulness became a part of me. We need these three components to feel totally, completely connected and, when we are, we live in total complete joy. Every experience can be enjoyed to its fullest extent because of this total connection. We see the beauty in absolutely everything, even a cloudy rainy day. We see the beauty of the energy that it took to form whatever it is. I'll give you an example of the joy I feel in an experience.

On the Labour Day weekend 2010, I drove to the west of here at night on a high mountain pass highway. It was very winding and it was like driving a rally road, cutting corners to keep the flow of the drive going, without braking too much.

As I was driving my head and cheeks were on fire and I said to Spirit, "You're really enjoying this aren't you?" And Spirit laughed back at me saying, "This is a lot of fun ha, ha." I hadn't driven a road like that in years and it was a real rush. The communication is now clear and free flowing and, like I said, I just enjoy my experience. Because that's what it's all about my brothers and sisters; enjoy the ride!

This communication is concise and very precious. It's in thought not vocalized as it was at first. These thoughts are of words or images in my mind. Before it was words and Spirit would speak to me out loud.

Having this clear, concise and authoritative thought allows me to be very confident in any subject matter. Any question is usually answered in a few short minutes if not seconds.

Having this free flow of knowledge gives us the ability to speak on any subject. That confidence gives us the total package of trust, love and faithfulness and, as I said on the last page, creates total joy in our lives, with this full understanding of how awesome, magnificent and blessed this entire experience is. In turn, with that understanding, we begin to become a master in our life and can show others the joy. Also, understanding the simplicity is the entire game because we are the divine made manifest. With all the worry, stress (both physical and mental) and the lack of trust removed from us, we become a different person entirely. We cannot go back after this is understood. This joy is so incredible we want to tell the whole world but cannot because most cannot hear. This joy is the definition of bliss!

Here's another example of my open communication. In the summer of last year, 2010, I had a thought or a remembrance of what I call the "I am that I am" moment. We become conscience, not I but the entire we. It was a point of light in my mind which grew and grew in knowledge until it had understood everything.

Another was when I was lying on the couch watching a movie one morning. I fell asleep and then I woke, my body that is, just before Spirit returned. As it returned I felt the total bliss of the union of spirit with body. I couldn't get over it for hours. I now feel spirit enveloping my body, not jerking or jumping on like others do, and this feeling is very peaceful. When those things happen, it is a constant reminder that "I am that I am". All these things combined remind me of the faithfulness that I now have and, as I said, nothing will change that.

I'd like to go back just a bit here. As I had said, this communication only became trustworthy to me when I was writing Book 1. At that point I was still not changing my old habits. These habits were watching politics and listening to late night radio and other talk radio shows. These things interfered with my communication because of the negative energy that they create. Remember most of the things they talk about are from the past or look to the future. They do not stay in the present or the now of things.

I stopped those things, and started listening to music for most of the next six months as I was working. But, since the middle of August 2010, I have not had a radio on while I worked, only working with my thoughts. And I can say the energy level has improved very much and is sustaining me all night. Previously, for many months, it was only for part of the night. This also gives me joy because the thoughts, when connected to Spirit and Universal Mind, are always positive, light. Dark or negative energy cannot stay in the mind.

# 7 The Three-Headed Snake

I have touched on the one part of the three-headed snake as I call it, science. This three-headed snake is the one that blocks our joy because it knows all the rules to the game and knows there are no rules and no consequences to its actions. So it does what it does to enhance the lives of those in this elite group of people. This three-headed snake is headed by the kings (royalty of all types, lords of the land) the priests (religions of all faiths) and the scientists.

At the beginning of this civilization the king ruled all that his armies could conquer and the spoils of war were all the riches of the land, including the people who were enslaved in one way or another, paying high taxes to the king. The king would live an unfettered lifestyle no matter the circumstances that befell all others in the kingdom. This king was the unchallenged head of the kingdom with his priest and the astronomer or seer (scientist) at his beck and call. The enslaving of the people was simple at first because the armies of the king were powerful and could keep the people in line. As things progressed, the grip became weaker. So other tactics had to be applied to enslave the people. It became a mind game to create fear. It wasn't purely a matter of brute force as in the past. The might didn't work as well.

Along comes the priest with his deities for whatever the circumstances: sun, moon, water, rain, land, etc. and these deities need to be pacified in some way or another. This probably involved some type of sacrifice by the people, giving up something—part of their crop or an innocent one—to calm some deity of nature.

That created fear amongst the people that their actions were somehow connected to the prosperity of the land, their crops dying, no rain, etc. This fear gave power to the priest and other fear-based religions grew from these basic ideas.

I'll give you an example of how religion creates fear or negative energy. In late August of 2009 I went to a church which I was invited to by another golfer I met in May of 2009. He told me that they teach the true teaching of Jesus, so I went thinking this would be a different experience. At first it was very positive with lots of music and dancing and singing, and the energy was flowing very well. I was still in the afterglow of my physical changes. Then later, after the music was over, a speaker came to the front and started on the negative and religious teachings. I felt physically sick, I couldn't walk out, I was in the front row with my acquaintance. I had to leave as soon as I could, and it took me three or four hours to recover from the negative energy.

One day, in the summer of 2009, in the small church where I worked, I saw a white board in the pastor's office. It was used to teach the elders and the youth of the church how to teach the word to others. It said focus on the word (of the Bible) and make sure that other ideas or thoughts do not enter your mind. Basically it is telling people to think what they are told rather than trusting their own experience.

I'm not attacking anyone here. There are some very beautiful people in this church and other religions. I'm only pointing out things I've observed.

Most cultures have a metaphor for the fall of humankind. This metaphor in western civilization is Adam and Eve, in the garden, being urged by a snake or serpent to eat from the tree of knowledge. Then humankind somehow became cursed.

This is the actual interpretation. Adam and Eve are the yin and yang or male and female (opposites, the dichotomy), the garden is the magnificence of perfection, the snake is the knowledge and the tree of knowledge is the opposite of the perfection or the physical. So humankind or all beings of all kinds achieved the physical and the experience began. This was the original blessing of the universe.

The third part of this snake is science. As I described earlier, it creates fear and doubt by questioning our nature, telling us that there is something that we don't know and there's always something that's going to get us. The bogey man, some new discoveries, the planet's going to the dogs in one way or another.

These three things are controlled by the Royalty or heads of state. They work in concert with one another to create fear, doubt and lack of confidence in ourselves and create profit for them. They created a false doctrine to make it easier for them to justify their actions.

What is the false doctrine again?

1. The separation from god and each other allowing the hurtful things that we do to each other, allowing war, starvation and inequities of all kinds to be justified.

2. That we are bad or EVIL, allowing the killing and security machine to operate as a correcting mechanism for this flaw that we can never overcome, and therefore we cannot live in harmony.

3. That we own anything: other people, husband, wife, child, pet or that we own land and that owning land is our birth right.

As you can see these three things are a constant problem in today's world, creating all the problems that keep us (the majority) from experiencing our joy.

Let's take them one at a time. The separation from god and each other is accomplished by dividing the people up by first telling us that god either doesn't exist or that It is somewhere off on a cloud someplace. Allowing us to be put in fear by the methods that they all use (all three of them). Example: God is a judge therefore we must watch out in all that we do, and that there is a good place and a bad place we could all end up in when we pass. We have created opposites by creating a character that is totally false, without any merit even in a logical mind. A serpent or snake is the symbol of knowledge in all cultures yet Christianity makes the serpent a symbol of evil and temptation. It is not even plausible that the All of Everything would have a rival such as this. It's just plain laughable. Yet we have entire cultures that believe this to be true and live in the fear created by it. Remember fear is the opposite of love. This is the dichotomy. Fear is the illusion created by us in our mind because we do not remember the truth.

Therefore this allows the division of all, the separation from each other; because we believe that each other's actions are a result of this false illusion of the serpent of temptation, therefore justifying it. Justifying that we are bad and that we need to be separated from each other in all ways: religion, culture, colour, all classes of people are separated. Then this is used to justify killing, starvation and the total inequities of this world.

Despite what we believe in the west, that we are an advanced society, we still live in a class based society with many levels of prejudice. It's ingrained in us through our religious teachings, education and leadership.

This is a direct result of the three-headed snake and their constant programming over the centuries. The kings and other royalty classified the people, and they were treated differently according to their class. This was done everywhere in the world. Then came religions which, by the way, had the monarch or head of state as the keeper of faith. The religions created the fear of god and one another. Then science dismissed the true parts of faith and created the "show me" state where no one could prove anything other than the physical, as I stated earlier.

Then there's the big one—the fear of death! We don't talk about it unless someone passes. We say passed and yet we don't know what that really means, do we?

Lack of understanding creates the fear of death but no one really knows do they? In some situations when I've talked about death as I have been shown it, I've been labelled and ostracized because people don't want to think about it. It's the great mystery! We are afraid to even ask, so we don't. That's why it's such a shock if a person like me knows something and tries to talk to someone about it.

With this fear in place, no one can discuss death and the understanding doesn't exist. The few people who understood the knowledge hid it from the masses who continue in fear. This enabled the elite to create the snake and to operate without question, making their lives more and more comfortable with the profits of the separation.

The ownership part is very straightforward. With the separation in place all things can be bought or sold including people and land. This also creates profit from the separation of people, creating war over the land and its resources. Sharing and equity do not exist.

Remember that these people, the elite, own shares in many large corporations dealing in the war and security machine.

Now how does religion profit from the mystery created by the false doctrine. The separation and the associated misery, created by the false doctrine, are very profitable for the religious machine. The followers of these religions give money to help out and support the religion but a very small percentage of the money ever makes it past the hierarchy of the church. It's used in propping up that institution. The result is many rich and powerful religious institutions.

How does science profit? By focusing on the doubt and constant questioning of everything. The state gives funding—there's always something to research—but if we knew the truth then that funding would dry up wouldn't it? So they all work against us and our ability to create confidence, trust and love and therefore creating the experience of joy in our lives. While the complete fullness of joy comes from the total understanding of the divine truth in us, not from the love, trust and openness, they are important in our evolution.!

This universal divine truth, or the understanding of it, is what creates the full complete joy in our lives. Because it creates certainty that life is not a waste, that it is a blessing to us and to All That Is. This certainty creates the purpose in our lives, understanding that the experience is our purpose and that we are no longer questioning, wondering, "What's the point? Why am I here?" And with that purpose comes a passion for the experience, a zest for all things in the experience.

But remember that these observations about the three-headed snake are only here for your awareness, they need not affect your experience. Remember that it does not matter about them unless we allow it to. W are the creator and the created so we can create anything that suits our experience.

# 8 All the Prophets

As I stated earlier, when we understand that this experience is only a game, a movie, a play, created by our choices, then we will reach mastery. This is what the elite do, play this game and use their understanding to profit off the backs of the majority. Now a majority of the royalty or elite know this. They live very well as a result and they teach all their children the rules of the game.

This is where the prophets came from. They were the children of the nobility who wanted to share their knowledge with the others in their kingdoms. All the major prophets were from this line of royalty despite what the holy books say. This included Confucius, Krishna, Rama, Mohammed, Buddha, Jesus and Moses. This is why every religion's basic teachings are the same; they all got their teachings from the same sources. And that's how all the religions were based on these prophets' teachings. They never intended to start any major followings, they just wanted the truth to be told to the masses and to release them from the bonds of fear and slavery that their families had created. The religions were created by the elite as tools, taking the prophets' teachings and twisting them to their benefit.

This, in turn, gave them even more control, creating a god who, for the most part, was a representation of themselves; a ruler, a judge, a tyrant, something else for the people to fear.

All the prophets wanted to be totally disconnected from their family line because of what they learned and how their fathers used their power against the people.

This is why the prophets generally (there were exceptions) lived a peasant-like lifestyle, becoming one with the people they were trying to help lift up and creating a more acceptable platform from which to teach. If they had come out as they truly were, they would have been rejected as Jesus was rejected in his hometown.

All of this knowledge was simple and easy to teach. Because of its total simplicity, it spread very quickly through the mass of people. But as always, as I stated in the last paragraph, this was the reason for the takeover of early Christianity by the Roman Empire. They high jacked it to continue the Roman Empire for hundreds of more years. The same was done in the other religions. Simply put, the teachings of the prophets were so simple that they had to be stopped and the message changed and complicated, in order for the status quo to remain. We still do this today with all aspects of the three-headed snake. Remember that the original version of the New Testament of the Bible was only thirteen pages long, one page for each disciple and an epilogue. I've really gone deep on this compared to them. We have put the men ahead of their message so the message got lost. This was also done on purpose by the elite. Today we do the same with our fallen prophets like, Martin Luther King Jr.,

John Lennon and Bob Marley to name just a few. Mainly their message is lost by the image of the person.

# 9 Being Human

That's what we are, being human or a human being. We come into our body to be human. Sounds too simple, doesn't it? The reason I say this is that even after having reached the point of understanding and total knowing, there are still days that I am totally human. My energy is there, but I don't bring it up or meditate, whatever you want to call it. I have all the frailty of a human. I feel pain etc, but that's my fault. I'm just lazy some days. But the energy is always there, the feeling of loving all of it. I just become a little too laid back and sometimes it's hard to be what we are in this world of non believing people. The fear never enters my mind though. We just are so I let down my guard a bit.

Sometime it's difficult to be human because you don't want to feel the frailty of this existence. I prefer to be all that I am. The knowledge is very empowering to everyone. Allowing doubt in just doesn't work because we can't change who we are. I want to experience all that being human is since the last twenty-five years have been as a working machine sixty-five to seventy hours a week. The knowledge, everything combined, makes up the experience.

I had mentioned in Book 1 about feeling that the energy is always there. We all seek this energy because we want that feeling we had as small children. I did it through my addiction to work. I'd get high on the energy after a few hours. Others seek it through their work, sporting life as a player or a fan, through their sex life be it normal or as an addiction. Other addicts get it from drugs, alcohol and gambling. Since I have the energy and it is always there, I do not seek it in my work anymore. It's just part of me.

There are other ways which we seek the energy. We seek it from others, that being the spirits of other beings or things. We seek out a tree on the street to eat our lunch under, we go to the park and sit by a rock. Then there is our so-called call to nature. This is our natural seeking of the energy that all living things give us. We head for the hills, so to speak. We climb mountains, go camping, hiking, all these things involve us in seeking out the energy of all living beings. They rejuvenate us because we take in their energy. This is how we are supposed to live—with nature, not in concrete cities.

So this is how everything works, even in the city and even if the thing is not alive as natural things are. We send our focused thought out and Universal Mind contacts the spirit of that which is living to manifest our request; but if it is not alive Universal Mind, All of Everything, sends out it's vibration to make that thing work for us. Remember that Universal Mind or God is light, and this vibration is a spinning light of thought which makes the thing work. It Which Is, is the coordinator, and we are the experiencer. Everything is a vibration of light. And that vibration is our thought made manifest because everything in existence is thought made manifest. Therefore our will is It's will made manifest. So if we mind (focus your thoughts) then everything matters (thought energy turned into matter) but if we don't mind then nothing matters. Gene Redenberry coined the phrase, "My mind is your mind and your thoughts are my thoughts". This is essentially what is our complete nature.

Some people say that what happened to me was a miracle, but if you understand what I just said then you will understand that I made a choice. I was given enough information to create a miracle or manifest my will by asking for what I truly desired. Remember everything is about creating. The name for these books is creating and that was given to me by Spirit before I totally understood what I was writing about. We create everything in our lives by the choices that we make. Those choices create everything that we are. This is why we know that choice is in everything that we do or attempt to do in our experience. We cannot not choose. It is the essential part of the creation. We cannot create without first conceiving a thought, which is a choice. We decide what we want first, then ask for it, then it's manifested. Nothing is given to us that we did not choose first.

I will give you an example of how I created my experience and enjoyed it. This is what I mean about living with certainty, purpose and passion.

My family and I have just returned from a trip to Southern Ontario on the Thanksgiving long weekend in Canada as I am writing this.

A week before we went I said this prayer. Thank you Father/Mother for moving this high pressure that's in BC right now down to Southern Ontario (we had been having warm above seasonal weather that week). I said it three times as per usual. And I left it, trusted, gave it away. I saw that the weather had been quite wet that week but on the Friday it changed and all weekend it was beautiful, between 20 and 22°C. We totally enjoyed our trip to Niagara and saw the Great Lakes and all the other beauty from the air on our flight because of the beautiful weather. We know many things about Niagara Falls, Southern Ontario and the Great Lakes from books, TV etc. But experiencing it was a total rush. This is our essence, experience. It knew everything but had no experience. We experience, for It Which Is. The whole trip was worth it when we put Rachel up to the railing at Niagara Falls and all she said was, "Woooow," for three seconds.

# 10 Don't Taint My Experience

As I stated earlier the three-headed snake uses a lot of doubt and fear to create our lack of confidence in what we are, therefore keeping us in bondage. Here are a few other ways that they use, for you to be aware of on your journey to compete joy.

The news media uses negative and fear based stories over 90% of the time, broadcasting or writing stories of death, destruction or things about diseases that may affect you. At the turn of every page, dial and web page, the media tells us that there's something out there that we need to be afraid of. Remember, always remember, nothing can get us. This negative influence is easily avoided by simply turning it off. If it doesn't affect your life than why watch or consume it.

Take in the essential information that pertains to your life then shut it off!

The other big one is magazines, newspapers and electronic media that cover celebrity so-called news or gossip. These things again do not affect our lives, they are another mechanism to diminish our experience. Remember, everyone chooses their experience, no one experience is better or worse than any other. The celebrity life is not as good as it's portrayed. It has its bad side too, the dichotomy of everything, remember. But this has an effect on people. Some cannot get enough and it becomes an obsession for them.

Their lives or experiences are not ours. Ours is as unique as each of the snowflakes falling from the sky. This is why we are here. Do not allow others' experiences to taint yours. Remember, we are the experience of All That Is and It experiences through us! This is our purpose fully and completely. This is why we have a zest for our experience. Enjoy the experience! What is your mantra? Mine is "Nothing will ever defeat me". Earlier in life it was "No retreat, no surrender". Other people's are "No worries," "It's all good," "No fear," "It's all in the experience," "Blessed is he or she who trusts in the Lord". All these mantras are based on the principles which I've laid out in these books. Always remember: all is divine, all is good, all is moving forward. We are the blessed of the divine. Our experience is totally blessed and we live in all the blessing that we bring to ourselves in our experience. So be blessed in your experience and know that every step of the experience is the experience!

Our birthright is to live in total joy in our experience as the small child does. We are here to live in that joy although we've had our experience tainted by the efforts of those who choose to keep us in the dark. But by shining a light on those who do so, we can bring more people into the light of their true experience, thereby helping others to enjoy their experience and creating a more just society in turn. Highly evolved beings want to live in harmony with justice for all.

# 11 It's All Good

You must be asking yourself, is this guy real? Since his experience has it been all good? No, I'll give you an example. Dispute all the good, there are challenges, but I never stop trusting. This past summer (May-August) I had a very big challenge to overcome. My loved one made a choice that affected all of us in our family. I choose not to totally separate from the family so I could be close to Rachel every day. So I moved into the basement and had to renovate it.

I had no savings to do this but I trusted, never allowing myself to get angry or upset because I understood that everyone has their path. I respected her as a highly evolved being. My ego is no longer with me since my clearing. This is why having this understanding changes you. I had a good summer learning more and understanding more. By the end of August we were a family again. I never let my trust go; understanding that going with the flow is the only way to be.

A lot of people say, "It's all good." Then they ask, "How is it all good when you look at the world?" I've explained what our experience is, but one has to gasp it. As I explain it, in being human we seek the energy that we had as a small child. This seeking causes us to do things that we would not do if the universal truth was taught to all. There would be an understanding and equality for all, and this need would not exist in a society based on those truths.

Here is an example of what we would do differently if this were the case. Loved ones would not force their very ILL (if people even got very ILL) and elderly people to stay with us.. And the medical community would be focused on healing rather than making money by perpetuating illness. With understanding the truth of this experience, people would not need to get ill to die. If they chose to leave they could do so freely instead of hanging on at all costs. When we understand that; when doubt, fear, and lack of confidence are gone; nothing matters and, even if no one believes us, we've still won the game. Then nothing will matter because we are good with what is and will never change.

So we say stay in the light and if we stay in the light understanding will come to us eventually. By trusting, the love will come, with the love the faithfulness will come and by living our experience, we will create the joy! With that joy we will create certainty, and with the certainty will come purpose and passion for the experience. Love the experience and live in joy!

# Book 3
# Creating Instant Truth
# Manifesting Our Love

# Introduction

As I have said in both previous books, this is not an attempt at writing the great spiritual book. It is about telling the truth about who I am and to help you know who you are through my example. Remember, everything is an example for us to follow. We just need to look, listen and feel it within us. By using myself I am bringing all the knowledge together, 1+1+1= come together. As the Beatles said, "There is nothing new under the sun." As I've stated, let's focus, or choose to focus, our attention on these truths. They are there for the eyes to see and ears to hear. I'm just a regular guy who has experienced the truth and wants my fellow humans to see, feel and experience what I have. I lack nothing in my life. I don't need this to make a living at. I do very well in my business. But if circumstances change, as everything always does, my passion for this subject may change my course.

In this book I'll talk about how we can manifest or bring about change in us. Without balance within, we can not change the circumstances which we see and effect positive change in the world around us. I'll give some suggestions on how we can change, as in the first book, interpretations of some prophecies as well as anything else that comes forth from me in the flow of writing. As I said in the other books, my thought from Sprit is instant, no meditation required. I just focus my thought and I'm connected without my filter getting in the way. That is where the "Creating Instant" comes from.

# 1 Help You Believe

In Book 1, I talked about the basics, about how we can change our vibration or speed of thought by experiencing—creating and conceiving. As I said, I did this fairly easily and with the help of Spirit it didn't take much work. I just did it and that is what you can do. Just be it. If you want to change your experience, do it. Put the thought into what you want/crave/desire.

Create the experience you want by acting like you are who you are and reinforce that every second of the day until you totally believe it. Don't keep changing your mind on who you are. Some call it constant prayer. I call it focused thought. Run the concepts in these books or *Conversations with God* through your mind and focus on that and only that all day, until you know what you are and the doubt, worry and fear are totally gone. Look for the triune (holy trinity) in everything around you as well. Street signs, company names, slogans, etc. Even with my experiences, I had to do this to overcome the Divine Dilemma. Those experiences and my physical changes were my backup to support me against all the doubt that the world throws at us.

First of all, I try not to watch too many newscasts or negative stories on TV, TV series that have stories of killing, abuse, etc. Those things tend to play on my mind.

Stay away, if possible, from competitive sports because of the war-like atmosphere or lack of equity they create between teams, cities or countries. Believe me, competition creates a war-like attitude. Remember we are total equals. Winning and losing is not equal. You might say it's just sport. But if you listen to the broadcasts, they're very much based on war, and they condition the mind in that way. If you play sports, play only as entertainment. As I said, I play golf, which is just me and the course.

I tried to play in a tournament with a good friend in October 2010, and I played worse than I had in many years. I figured out only afterward that it was because I put expectation on myself or worry, which caused negative energy, and my body wouldn't function correctly. I had been playing well up to that point in the season.

Avoid the political game as well. It's all inequity, too. Parties are win/lose. No one is on your side. They work for the elite.

Try to stay away from dark themed movies, books, plays, etc. Especially slasher movies, war movies and ones with a lot of violence. As your fearful thoughts and your programming of the false doctrine are eliminated, you can move back to those things because you understand that they are simply a story. But until all the negativity is out, try not to put more in. That's a key to clearing out those things.

For the time that you are cleansing your mind, stick to positive up-beat music, mainly music that flows, not any music that the beats move in more than one direction at once. That always creates negative energy. The music I listen to is mainly Classic Rock from the late 60s to early 90s and maybe even the early 2000s. There is a lot of spiritual music in that genre. In some of those songs I hear references to experiences similar to mine. It seems that they don't want to be marginalized so they write it in their song lyrics. I've asked people about certain songs and they cannot hear the lyrics or recognize the meanings.

Keep it in the key of C, F, G, C, with a beat of 1, 2, 3 — The Holy Triangle remember.

I watch a lot of movies for entertainment. I look for positive movies, again with spiritual and power of thought themes. There are a lot of movies out recently about how thought creates things in the hearts (mind) of humans. Science fiction, fantasy. A lot of these movies are mostly positive.

As well, simply act like a happy, well-balanced, highly evolved person (a person who puts out love) and treat everyone with total integrity, honesty and truth, smiling and saying, "Have a good (or great) day," no matter what the circumstances. This creates the sense of connection with others, creates positive energy in you and sends it to others. Live in the now, enjoying this second with the knowledge that you are an everlasting being and that this second, or few seconds, is all that exists.

Worry is for those who are concerned about their existence, their future. When we understand who we are, we are ensured of our future and anything we desire will be given if we ask and follow the criteria laid out, knowing it and believing as all the masters have taught.

I'm going to revisit an earlier point about competitive sport and how it affects our thoughts. In almost all areas of the world, there are fanatical sports fans. Why this is promoted is one of the major points of these books. It's about creating a culture of negative collective thought. As an example, in Canada it's hockey creating a culture of winning and losing, competitiveness at all turns, game to game. Even between games and between seasons, the collective community is focused on this. There is absolutely no letup. There is a positive side to sport as in all things. Teamwork, getting along with others, personal growth, but it is not necessary to create a win/lose attitude in the kids, especially when it programs them for a system. This creates belief in everyone's mind that life has to be this way, winning and losing, power and control over everybody and creating a collective thought of not thinking for ourselves. It's centred on the group. That's fine if there is equity, but equity doesn't exist. It's an elitist way of living. Soccer and rugby in Europe and cricket in Asia predominate the culture. This goes for our educational culture as well, and it creates the negative energy that we feel because it's not what we are. That is the heaviness that I referred to in Book 2. It weights us all down.

I'll give you an example of this fanatical thought. I was watching a play-off hockey game in May 2010 with the local professional team playing in game 2 against their opponent. The locals were up 2-0 in the second period, carrying the play against a favoured team and leading the series 1-0. I got a very bad headache and I, to that point, hardly had headaches since the change. The opponents scored and the headache cleared. At that point I knew the locals would lose the game and the series, which they did. Later than night I figured this was again the mass consciousness worrying about the team. If I felt that, imagine how the team felt. It weighed them down so they couldn't perform to their abilities.

I had this happen during the West Kelowna fires of the summer of 2009, in January of 2010 the day of the Haitian earthquake and recently the day of the New Zealand earthquake. When there is stress in the mass consciousness, I feel it. I am what you call an ultra sensitive. This shows the power of mass consciousness. When people are stressed, their negative thoughts are heavy and we all can feel them.

This energy is created in all cultures by all the things I just mentioned, and also by all the actions of the three-headed snake. This is the bondage that we are all under. As I have been saying throughout, thought is everything!

All the negative patterns and behaviours are part of our education and have created a culture of repeat, repeat, repeat. Therefore the mistakes, or sins, of the past are put on the children and their children, thus allowing no real evolution and, for many, this pattern continues.

Here is an example. I was playing with Rachel and she got very aggressive and was scratching me. I said, "You're a tiger." She responded, "I'm not a tiger." This is the child saying, "This is only my opposite. I am love." She was expressing the dichotomy. This is an example of how we program our children. If we keep calling them tigers, they will believe they are tigers. Because of my awareness, I immediately stopped referring to her in this way?

I remembered that my father had called me dull and slow when I was young. Then my brother and other kids picked it up, and that's what I became—a dullard. I believed it so strongly that it became true—at least in my mind. You may recall that I referred to myself as a dullard at the beginning of this book.

Since we now have the knowledge I'm sharing, we can reprogram ourselves and hope that the mainstream catches up with us and changes everything for everyone!

Remember to focus on knowing that we are the highest form of thought and emotion rather than our cultural focus totally on the body which keeps thoughts weighted down.

Since we are talking about mass consciousness, I promised to complete the circle. I'll give you a few examples of how the unfocused thoughts of mass consciousness work, as opposed to an individual's specific focused thought.

I use weather examples a lot because they are what I do better and they are measurable and observable. Back in Book 1, I told you about the winter of 2009 here in the Okanagan of British Columbia, what I asked for and how it played out. The mass consciousness became focused and pushed away what I had originally asked. In the spring people began to worry about another drought year. On the May, 2010 quarter moon, about the 12th, I asked to alleviate the drought situation here in the valley. For the next month or 40 days, until the last part of June, it rained and was cool. The snow in the mountains didn't melt, the creeks and lakes had enough water and in the summer there was no a drought.

In Saskatchewan, they had a very similar situation and in June and July it rained and rained and rained, too much rain. I figured everyone was asking for rain unconsciously and they got it. The crops couldn't be planted in some places and others died in the field.

Here is another example. In the summer of 2009, I was listening to that late night radio show again. There was a guest on talking about intent and they asked the listeners to pray for a certain south-eastern US city which had extreme drought. Then in July of 2010, I was listening again and they talked about the flooding in that city. It was very bad. It had taken a year to manifest itself.

Here's one of the points I was talking about, when we have a" theory" about something it may be something that we maybe kinda believe. This is why I practiced on the places away from populated areas until I totally understood what I was doing. The mass consciousness can produce anything if it is unconscious, even while not understanding its power. Even if they kinda believe, it can be a bit dangerous. But nothing matters. It's just a point of reference for you to ponder.

Also, this past winter, 2010-2011, all of North America was supposed to have an extreme winter. A few people I know in British Columbia asked for a gentle winter and it manifested. There have been probably no more than five very cold days here and only five big snow falls. In the rest of North America that hasn't been the case. It's been cold with lots and lots of snow, especially on the east coast. The experts were telling people this would happen so the mass consciousness believed and unconsciously asked for it. I use these examples with people all the time to explain how thought works and how the universe really works. These examples are easy for people to reference in their minds and makes the principle very simple to explain.

I will now continue with the things I did to deprogram myself. I focused on the spinning light that comes out from the third eye. I'll explain that. When I look at something solid, a wall, desk, floor, etc, between my eyes is a very small spinning circle. It looks like a mini galaxy, a spiral of light. This is my light shining out of the third eye. When I first wake up, it's clear. As I fully awaken it becomes smaller and more distorted, but I can find it any time throughout the day. I've seen it since I was a child but I didn't know what it was. It is this spinning light that cleared out my negative thoughts on May 9th, 2009. Try looking for this spinning light. It may work but you must believe in what you are. Breathe way back, back, back with your eyes closed and allow everything to flow. Don't try too hard. It's all flow remember. All I did was want my head to clear of the heaviness that I was still experiencing, and it just happened. But all these things are based on belief, total belief in who and what you are and the process you are in. Focus on that and you will be successful. The masters only said, "Believe in Self, believe in your actions, believe in your emotions." Here is one other thing on manifesting with focused thought or prayer. As I wrote this at the end of January, 2011, I had recently started to say, "I am," and "It doesn't get any better than this," to help focus. When I say the prayer for everything I encounter in my life, I acknowledge, accept and bless it. Because everything is blessed, for all is the oneness.

We can live unconsciously and allow the doubt, fear and pain of the false doctrine run our lives. Or we can have the courage it takes to live consciously and live with total balance and equity in our life, thereby allowing us to help create a better world with balance and equity for all. You have heard the term, "on the road to nowhere". That is where we are, now here. At the very beginning did I not say this is one of the mansions in the kingdom of heaven? So let's manifest a change to make this an improved place to live. I don't know about you but I want to come here a few more times. It's a nice place and every earth is likely different from this one. So let's try to work together on changing this earth to a place where you or I can return to any place or time and have a good equitable experience.

# 2 Understanding Your Spirit

I've talked about changing the thought patterns we've been programmed with or are reprogramming ourselves with. Let's talk about understanding how we distinguish between our ego and spirit thought. There is a difference. This is the part I mentioned in Book 2 about faithfulness or faithful communication with ourselves.

The brain is the transmitter and receiver of thought, as I said before. We put thought into our memory or ego mind as a computer gets base programs into its microprocessor. We fill our ego mind with those thoughts. Good, bad or otherwise those thoughts become who we are in the physical. Our brain has three parts, like everything else. The largest is the transmitter and receiver in the top of the brain, That which is. Then there's the middle That which is being or spirit. The smallest part is the operator of our body functions and ego mind, That which is experiencing.

These three parts are what make up our thought matrix. "Three is one" as I have said throughout.

Again the ego mind is the smallest and most predominant part in the physical experience. Think of these thoughts as our lower thoughts, thoughts of the physical needs, wants and desires. When we become connected to spirit thought, these thoughts are of a higher being or the highest being, That which is being. This is our higher self, our source inside speaking to our physical self. It's simpler than that. The higher self is that voice telling us what to do in certain circumstances but in this case it becomes the voice which we talk to as our self. When we get to this level, it's a matter of understanding which voice we are talking to. Is it my ego or my spirit?

My experience was very simple because when my spirit took over for those few days, it was very predominant, and I knew which was which so I was one with it. Remember, everything is thought, emotion, experience. I'll simplify this for your understanding. The physical is the experience or ego. Emotion and thought are our spirit mind and our only connection with source is by the transmitter. It sends and receives our thought to source, sending out our focused thought. Though in my experience I have received some direct communication from Source as well. The examples are in Book 2 and this one.

This is our highest or grandest thought. That is the "I am that I am".

When it comes to understanding that voice in our head, grasping that faithful communication I speak of, it takes time. I ask myself what is my highest thought on some subject or emotion. Ask what would love do? How would love act in this situation. Understanding this thought is what we are about, doing things that come to us, not thinking or filtering it, just doing it. Acting out of first thought, first emotion, but not at a primal level as some do now.

Our actions are that action, highest or grandest. These things are innate to us. Choosing that grandest action is what we want to do.

Being able to distinguish this is what we want to do, following that highest thought and emotion. That's what I do because I believe in WHO I AM!

When we are first trying to do this, it's difficult to understand; but as with all things, practice makes perfect.

If you've been following along through the book, understanding this will be easier because you have started to change your thinking. When we change our thoughts, then we become those thoughts just as we've become all our previous negative thoughts. All forms of negative thought are very harmful to body functions, especially the brain, causing all kinds of problems for managing our heath. As I stated before about heavy energy, it affects the brain the most.

Now if our first thought is a reactive thought, we think again. Act like WHO WE ARE. Those reactive thoughts will, as I just stated, become less as we think about our actions and not react to any situation.

The way I did it, as I said in the last chapter, was to focus my thought on what I am. I mentioned my thoughts understanding everything that entered my mind, be it positive or negative, and filtering out those thoughts which I do not want in my mind. I created my thoughts so that I created myself not allowing those outside thoughts in. If they do, then I again filter, examine them, look at them and see if I want them.

That's what I mean by monitoring my thoughts. As well, in any process, this monitoring of thought enables us to clear our ego mind of thoughts, therefore allowing for easy simple meditation. There are no special requirements for this. It can be done any time and any where. I say, "I am love," and that brings in the energy.

This process took me a few months, but I had the advantage of my experiences as in all this process. When we reach this level of thought management, we are able to think in that God space that we all want to be in. This is the blissful space I talk about in Book 2.

How do we know that Spirit is talking to us? As I stated in Book 2, It communicates in an authoritative, conscious and precise way. The thought is generally something I asked about in my ego mind; the answers I receive are as above and without prior knowledge of the topic. I would ask a question that I had no idea about or had visions of things that under normal thought I wouldn't have known about. Like the big bang thought. In the summer of '09 I asked about gravity, and I got an explanation about how the earth was formed, fully and completely. I had no clue about these things. It was fully and completely in detail. I auto channelled it. At the time a lot of the things happened that blew me away. It was giving me a sample of Its knowledge to help me believe in myself. Also, when truth comes through, the energy flows; my fingers tingle and my feet burn with energy. Another thing is that Spirit will speak to me as my brother/sister. When Universal Mind comes in, and, as

I've mentioned it's not that often, it will be like MY CHILD! It's about a million times stronger than Spirit.

Bless the spiritual writers and speakers. However, believing someone else's teachings is where the disconnection comes from. Most seem to believe they are connecting to Universal Mind or Source, but if they have only theory and not experience, they are reinforcing the false doctrine of separation. It is the source within that tells us these things. Some teachers need to meditate to connect to Spirit. I connect directly and instantly.

And as I stated in Book 2, with this state of mind we become those thoughts, and our thought energy is blissful or joyful. That is the passion that I spoke of.

That thought energy carries us through our days and we can live in the now and in the joy. Then we can think of higher thoughts. These thoughts bring us pleasure because we connect to the oneness of everything. We understand what everything is, means and feels like. Our ego becomes muted. It's still there but very much under control. As well I will have a conversation with Spirit, and it could last two hours as the night passes. I will likely go in three directions about something and then settle on one part and write about it.

With this we enter a stage of openness, where we allow ourselves to think about how we can make a difference not only in our life but also in the lives of others. When we arrive here we understand that we do not have to hoard, envy or be greedy about anything because we are all one, and that we can create a world of equity and not lose anything in our life.

So you might be thinking, "This guy writes like he's Mr. Happy all the time and everything will work out if we just believe." It hasn't always been this way. I had done a lot of work on myself even before this experience happened, but I got seemingly no results. I used to listen and watch gurus of spiritual knowledge on the radio and TV, as I stated before but I did not get any of this information from them. I did not love myself at all, zero. I served others all my life, and all it got me was death. When I awakened I became a new person. I remembered some things on my own, other principals I remembered from all the studying I did. My experiences told me I was the most important person in existence, and from that I grew to where I could love myself. By doing that I loved my family and in turn everyone else. By you doing this work on self, loving, thinking, doing, you will change everything in your life and everyone around you. We are taught by everything in our lives that love is conditional. Yet love has no conditions. This is what I was shown and am through all these experiences.

Mr. Happy keeps coming back no matter what happens. When I smile my whole being, body smiles. I didn't get that from a guru. I am almost 47 years old and I feel like 17, though I might not look it on the outside. Before I was 45 going on 65 with only a brick wall in front of me, and I was approaching it quickly. That's why I'm Mr Happy, and I will not change that. Let's go forward and help everyone see the world like I do. I see everyone as they really are, a small child without their programming, a highly evolved being with a coat or layers of negative programming that just needs to be removed. That's the whole purpose of my approach in these books.

There are many people teaching theories and asking you to believe in them and their teachings (be it religions, science or spirituality). They sorta, kinda, but not totally and completely understand because they generally don't "know". They lack experience. They have a created belief (programmed by doing over and over). It covers the truth with only a few distorted truths or limited information.

Knowing is something that is already there. You only need to uncover it or be reminded about it. Spirit does this for us if we are listening, and once we start to listen then we begin to remember and understand, not learn or believe. It's a knowing within. It's the difference between painting over something to make it look good and the sculptor chipping at the stone and finding the statue inside. Keep chipping until you find yourself. Bless the gurus for opening the doors that kept us in the dark ages, that we all have been experiencing, and offering the possibility of thinking for ourselves.

# 3 Your Little Master

The masters have used the small child as the example as I have in these books. I give you things to observe for your example. Remember in Book 1, at the very beginning, I told you about Rachel, the child who is with me (remember no ownership of anything), at one year old comforting me as I started my change? She understood and communicated to me through nonverbal communication. Why do you think George Lucas, the creator of Star Wars, used a little person as the master? Watch the child (under five before the veil is dropped). Listen and observe. When they start to talk they repeat things three times, Yum, Yum, Yum or No, No, No, etc. These are things I saw or heard. The way they hold their hands as I indicated in Book 1. Rachel would do this at times, still does, to bring in energy. When young children walk, they glide across the floor with a very soft touch. They drop things without noticing. This happens to me as well. When they play they act out experiences, things they couldn't have known in this life. Play is also the spirit training the body how to function in this world. Repeat, repeat, repeat. Especially in play. Their high level of energy causes their fingernails to be like razors, they scratch themselves very badly at times. When they begin to talk, they repeat words three times as I just said. This continues as they begin to speak in phrases, three-word phrases.

When Rachel does something she always says, "I did it."

This is the experience, understanding it, knowing it and expressing it.

Some children have very red cheeks (mine are red as well) when active. It's not the cold because they are inside at the time. I saw this one day with a child at daycare. She hadn't been outside. Rachel doesn't like to wear socks or shoes at times. Energy goes out our feet, remember. Touch a child's face, hands, feet or head. They can be very warm or hot at times. They're very sensitive to temperature, especially hot or cold running water. Rachel says, "Bless me," when she sneezes. We didn't teach her that. She also says it when we sneeze.

Children roar at times a low huh! huh! noise as I told you I did in Book 2. They assert their will of course. They have an ego, too. There're not a clean slate to be filled. Notice that they use their strength in that little body when they desire to use it.

They speak a language which we do not understand. They will conduct a conversation in that language with full understanding of what they're saying. The experts say it's babbling, but is it really? We know better than that. They love unconditionally and have only two fears: falling, which is survival mechanism, and bad dreams, which even I get freaked out by. Sometimes because we die a lot in those dreams. I have remembrances of many deaths. Children understand everything. We don't have to program them to do things they know.

When the small child plays, it's total and compete fun, not just because they're a small child but because they know that it's all a game. When they fall, they cry and are up and about very quickly. Observe them when they sleep. The languages they speak in their sleep are not from this life and flow better than this one.

On December 27, 2010, when she was two and a half years old, Rachel sat down beside me and said to me, "I'm, I'm your Mamma's Mamma." Then she showered me with kisses like my dad's mom would. She spoke about everyone as if they were female at that point. As we come back in different lifetimes, we all stay together as family or loved ones.

All these things are present in the small child if we look and listen. You are in the presence of a master and you may not know it. Eyes to see, ears to hear!

Children are highly evolved beings so treat them as such. They are learning to understand the language and culture as well as how to use the body and their human ego.

If we treat them as a chattel, they will act as such. Treat them as they are and they will develop faster and become the person they are sooner. By treating them as if we own them, they will devolve and become how we treat them. I've seen it for myself in a lot of cases in the recent past as I observe other children's development in comparison to Rachel's.

Why do a lot of teenagers go out in the cold with few clothes on? It's the energy.

Then there are the over active kids who, the teachers say, cannot focus. It's because they already know and they can't tell the truth because the adults won't believe them

The medical profession has come up with a new one for adults who can't focus either. They call it adults' overactive brains. This is just the person's frequency changing. I'll tell you more about this a little later on. The little masters are our guides to overcoming the programming. They set the example for us. Follow if you choose to see and hear.

I have spoken throughout these books about how we seek the energy that we had as a small child.

I understood this in the physical sense and why we do this. Until recently I was able to describe the reason but not the how, why or purpose of this. Although I did get sick a couple times in the past two years, I had been in such good health and being for so long that I hadn't realized that the physical manifestation of the negative energy was in all of us. We speak of the veil of misunderstanding that's brought down to the child at age five. I had said to my employee friend back at the start of my evolutions that "the veil has been taken from thine eyes". What did I mean? When the membrane was lifted from my brain back in May 2009.

As I stated before about the heavy, dark, negative energy that is on all of us, this is the veil that is put on us at age five, or the physical. The small child is partly in the light and partly in the dark energies. As we evolve, that veil is lifted, and we see our light as I descried in the first chapter. And we find the middle way between the physical and spirit, or the emotion of who we are. This is our future, that of being in the middle. Knowing the physical experience while knowing our true light. The small child shows us the way. The people I described earlier, who have trouble focussing, their frequency change is that of the veil thinning and them not realizing it. Mine was eliminated totally instantly. That's the EVOLUTION we are on the way to. The veil is a tightness, heaviness or fog in the frontal lobe of the brain. It is there and was there in me and others. Most use a drug (sugar, caffeine) to release this in the morning to ease this tightness. This tightness is the physical.

As I described it in Book 2, it can be throughout our body as well.

Those without the veil release it very quickly after awakening if they need to. The small child is very adept at this.

The emotion of emotion, means we live by our own emotion but understand that love is the only emotion that matters. All emotions make up pure love as all colours make up the pure white light of what we are. The light is the spirit of what we are when we are highly evolved. As the small child, we live on our highest emotion, the emotion of everything is love. This is the process we are moving toward. Being as the small child, love.

# 4 Technology

A lot of people in today's world believe that technology is the only way for us to progress and the physical technology, or machines, are the only avenue for change. What compelled me to write these books was an article that I read in early February, 2010 in a local magazine. The article asked the question, "How and when will we evolve?" I happen to work for the person who wrote the article. He has a lot of books, magazines and articles in his office about how the human body can be enhanced by technology. Most of these articles and books are about physically enhancing the human body by outside means. Yet we have the greatest piece of technology that ever existed on this planet or the universe, our thought.

As I have spoken about, our ancient ancestors knew how to use their bodies to enhance this thought energy for everything, including building the greatest structures that still stand today. I'm not talking about the people who renovated these structures for their use as spiritual temples and tombs. I mean the pyramids, all the pyramids and other massive stone structures around the world. This was done by thought energy moving very large stones into place, places where human physical strength and beast could not. The Master said, "Tell the mountain to get out of my way."

This is what he was referring to—our thought connected to source energy can move anything as long as we have no doubt. The universes were built with thought and this building of stone structures of any kind would be simple in comparison.

Here is an example of thought moving the universes. On December 21, 2010, I reread the last chapter in *Conversations with God Book 1*. I turn to it every time I want a little reminder. That day there was a lunar eclipse, a full moon and the winter solstice on the same day. Three, remember, the holy triangle. It said that the evolution of the universe, the formation of everything, happened in a holy instant. Remember that thought is faster than anything humans have figured out yet. I read that early in the morning before I went to sleep. In the afternoon as I was working, around the time of the solstice and the rising of the moon, my energy got very high, my head was very hot as it had been with awareness and the infinity remembrance. It hadn't been like that in a long time. Then I remembered about the holy instant.

I thought and I experienced the creation. It was like a movie in super fast forward. Everything moving at the speed of thought. (10 trillion, trillion. Everything is thought.) Then it stopped at the beginning of human kind a few hundred thousand years ago. As I stated in Book 1, we have figured out the what but not the how or the why. Conceive—create—experience. Everything is experience and to understand we must experience. I asked Spirit later, "Is this many people's experience?"

It answered, "Very few have experienced what you have, especially all Three, awareness, infinity and creation!" Everything in our journey must be experienced to be understood.

As I told my mother (teacher), "We have just slowed it down, we cannot think as fast as the All of Everything." Everything is the speed of each individual's thought. Everything has happened the way science has laid it out for us, but it all happened in that holy instant — probably three to six seconds is a good estimate — as I stated above.

Since that day I have been even more conscious of my thoughts; I understand everything and am able to experience it by thought. Everything is thought made manifest, and I understand even more so now than ever. It is all in our creation. We are always creating, and remember, we are creating those experiences to give us understanding of everything in our life.

By understanding this we can use or create the pyramids as our primary source of electric energy to power our future. These structures were built not as monuments but as power receiving stations, power filling stations and substations for society's use. This isn't new information. The pyramids were built to last, made from carbon (stone) with a solenoid inside to collect the energy (quantum energy) with limestone or a crystal at the top to focus this energy. This energy is boundless and clean, no environmental damage required save the building or refitting of the structures. This quantum energy can also be used to neutralize other types of very dangerous elements which are currently in use.

As I just stated, technology is possible with thought, conceive—create—experience. This is how the world that we know now has been created.

People like Bill Gates and Mark Zuckerberg (Facebook founder) did not foresee the uses of their innovation, they only conceived and created it and the experience took place. They did not know how they would impact the world. All technology is built on this thought. No one knows the impact of their conceived thought.

As we are talking about physical technology in this early 2011, our bodies, being great organic machines, are able to do anything if they are in balance and running correctly. Witnessing finely tuned athletic abilities is a good example of the great machine that we are.

But if it is out of balance, great difficulties can arise, especially today in the period of the great advances of physical technology. We are a frequency of light energy and therefore the highest form of frequency of wave energy. This technology that we are so fond of today, wireless technology, is taking us out of balance with our bodies. The radio waves from these devices are affecting our sleep, awakening us literally, not only physically awakening but also awakening our spirits.

This sleeping disease, as I call it, is affecting millions on the planet as these waves bounce around. I talked about this in Book 1. This lack of balance is not being recognized by the people it's affecting or the people who treat it. It is causing many problems as it did in me.

As I said in Book 1, returning the balance is achieved by eating raw food, vegetables, fruits, nuts and water for about three weeks. Putting the carbon from the plants into our carbon unit and restoring the balance. I had also mentioned in Book 2 my diet in the weeks following the revival by my spirit. I also mentioned in Book 1 about the planet returning the carbon to the atmosphere to help rebuild the body of the earth so we can function better and be more balanced.

What's happening to people is: the body is not able to function because of the lack of sleep, therefore the Sprit mind takes over and the strength and clarity of mind, the high, gives the person the strength to get through the day. When they complete that day, the body crashes back to the physical (heavy) body.

The ego mind believes it was the body doing it so the imbalance in the body causes the body not to sleep again and again. But the sprit mind is in control, compensating for the lack of physical energy with thought energy.

Treating the imbalance with drugs, alcohol and sugar leads to more problems, as stated above. The only solution is returning the body to a balanced state. Does Spirit not say, "I will never leave you nor forsake you."

This is not a disease that needs to be controlled or cured. It is an imbalance, and it is also leading to the evolution of humankind. This is a transitional state which is very difficult. This is affecting many creative people and people who need to use their minds to do their job.

Some self medicate. I used caffeine in colas, several litres a week. Some people use other drugs. Then there are the chemical based drugs which killed my body and do the same to many others each year.

Of the people who are in transition, some of us will move forward and evolve to a higher state of being, a state which all of us may be in one day. Then there are the ones who may go back to their unconscious life and others who, out of fear, regress beyond that to an unfeeling state, as I did in 2005. My experience in 2009 was my third time through this process and, as I stated in the other books, I was lucky to have made the right choice.

This evolution may happen to almost everyone because of the technology affecting our frequency, like it did in the 30s with Nicola Tesla and his energy collecting towers that had to be shut down.

Some will lead through this process, some will happily follow these leaders and others will stay in the pack of the unconscious for the time being. So we should understand this process, respect those going through it and love them for helping others understand. The system would like us to minimize, marginalize and mechanize them back into the system. We are evolving and the best thing for us to do is love those going through the change because we may be next and we'll need their support.

We have a good future unlike our two neighbours, Mars and the planet, that was between us and Mars, which we now call the asteroid belt of meteors that have an orbit. Is it possibly a planet that was destroyed, maybe by us, in a very distant past? These three planets are in the good zone, not too hot, not too cold. Three is one.

All the models in education, government and all forms of creating an equitable society exist now. All that's needed is the will to put them to use on a global scale creating the equitable society or civilization. That is, living civilly as one nation. All technology is available to us to conceive, create and experience an evolved planet.

# 5 Land of Confusion

The reason I wrote these books in this style is because, as I stated at the beginning of Book 1, the mind gets confused or negative thought enters and confuses us. So I hope I didn't confuse you too much. I wanted to explain everything to you knowing you would understand these simple basic concepts. Because we do know everything, we just need to remember or be reminded. KIS keep it simple or, as the kids say when we don't keep is simple, TMI too much information.

I have observed that some others seem to speak or write in great detail to make one simple point. But the great masters did not need to do this. They spoke or wrote in the simplest terms because they knew we know. They were just reminding us of who we are. Some who take the more complex path, do it for the undoing of others. If they truly wanted the truth to come out, they would speak in simple terms. However, they may not totally understand these things so they use this complex path to explain their confusion. Confusion or complexity shuts down the minds of the majority therefore creating another level of separation. We the majority want to understand easily and simply, not having to interpret complex concepts created about simple principles. By simple speaking truth and not using the more complex path to truth it would help the general public understand more readily.

When I speak to people I spend two to three minutes tops talking to them on one point. The person generally gets it and thanks me for it. If I were to spend 20 minutes with someone, I could explain everything to them. This is what telling the truth is and it's different from talking about a theory with a detailed explanation to cover the lack of total knowing.

We are all seeking the same enlightenment, that is the light that is in us all. On the evening of February 12, 2011, I had a short nap. When I awoke, laying there on the bed with my eyes closed, in my forehead a light of a pale blue colour with a dark spot in it, came in and went. Then it came in two more times. This was my white light coming in and being distorted by the yellow of the overhead light that was on in the room.

The Monday morning previous, when I was trying to find my way to write this book and doubted myself, I woke in my body and I was stiff. A second later the bliss of reunion with Spirit happened again. Spirit does this when I doubt a little. This really does the trick. This is bliss like no other in the physical experience.

Back to the light that we all seek. We are all going to the same place. Think of it as a mountain we need to get over. The well used path is smooth and well trodden but goes under the mountain. You need a big flashlight, and there are lots of dark corners and pitfalls along the way. The ones who have some enlightenment walk a narrow canyon with lots of rocks and boulders to trip over and very little light gets in. Then there are the totally enlightened whose climb is difficult but they cross the mountain. They walk freely through meadows of flowers with the sun shining brightly on their faces. Few take this path.

Let's look at some of the differences that some commonly held theories have compared to what I have stated. Let's hope I have filled the gaps that I promised at the start.

- Theory says the quantum energy is one and has only one source
  - The big bang energy is never created or destroyed, opposed to all the energies of all of us are always creating
- The theory is that there are healers that can heal people.
  - No one heals, they can only invoke your spirit to heal yourself
- Theory says that there is only one and that we are only an extension of the one and only, a puppet of the controller believing in only mind and body
  - We are a three-part being—triune, mind, body and spirit.
- The theories rarely mention the principles of the working of the universe, how they work and how to use them
  - I am providing the "how to".
- Theory says ask and receive with no doubt.
  - They don't give the detail on focused thought, how it actually works

- There is a theory that we are one and that equity should be given. Not much is mentioned of the programming or the false doctrine.
  - How can we remove the separation when no one mentions it and how it is created and nurtured.
- No mention of physical and mental changes
  - Most do not have any or, if they do, very little
- That when they connect to Spirit they believe it to be Universal Mind and that the information may slip away so it is written in a form that runs on and on.
  - They believe in the separation and not in the all knowing spirit within
- No understanding of the reason behind everything
  - The experience provides understanding
- No mention about minimize—marginalize—mechanize
- Some say they see colours of energy
  - Not many feel the energy
- They mention living in the now and that everything is, was and will be
  - They have no understanding in physical terms or experience
- Theory says awareness is a very slow process
  - I've outlined the three levels of awareness
    - First is the authoritative voice or images in the mind which we don't understand
    - Second is going to the light and not really understanding

- Third is the body dying, or other traumatic events happening, being revived by spiritual energy and having total and complete awareness, instantly. These are the three levels of awareness.

Theory is not understanding because it is only in the seeing of the physical things around us or the thought that became theory. Theory does not feel or experience things to fulfill the circle of knowledge. Experience is total understanding. This is the path to enlightenment.

One of the masters said that we need to struggle to find true enlightenment. But if, instead of being taught theories—either by design or by not understanding,—the truth were taught from the beginning, then the struggle would not be required because once the truth is told, a person can foster or nurture the truth in themselves and find their path without the struggle. This struggle of light over darkness is told in all our myths and legends. No matter how complex the story line, everything breaks down to light overcoming the darkness in us all. The False Doctrine is what makes finding enlightenment a struggle. Life was not designed to be a struggle. It was to be an expression of love to everyone. I have made a full circle in the writing of these books; the first is the emotion of the experience, the second is the emotion of thought or thought energy and the third is the emotion of emotion, which is what we are. Understand that this is our compete SELF. Once we achieve this, then we can finally move forward. That is all of us.

On March 11, 2011, the day of the Japanese earthquake, I was awakened by an odd feeling. Then a wave of emotion like a release, unlike anything I have yet to experience, washed over me. All I could say was, "WOW." It was the end of my physical change of not sleeping properly and changing back to the lightness I had at the beginning, going full circle back to May 2009.

Have you ever looked up at the moon or the stars with awe?

I look at the moon at it's zenith at night and I see what God really looks like. That pure white light is what God is. That's you looking at you. That's your light, your energy. This is why the gods of the religions of old were sun, moon and stars. Even the modern day religions and the flags of modern day use these symbols. We all seek the light that's inside of us.

Those who are truly seeking their light should seek out those who are of honesty, integrity and truth in their words. Those whose understanding is not complete, bless them for their effort and use what you will of their teachings to foster your light. They may write all these books in search of the truth that they are seeking in themselves. But if you seek universal truth, then seek a master teacher who only teaches in simple terms to enlighten. The other path is theirs and their truth may lead them to total enlightenment one day. But as I stated several times, because of my experiences, I am being, feeling and experiencing All That Is. Those who have had similar experiences do not speak or, if they do, their work is misinterpreted. They feel the marginalization that the world puts on free thought. Remember in Book 2 about the bubble of love, most eastern religions speak of the circle inside the circle inside the circle.

This, in my experience, is the bubble around me, the earth and all the universes. The bubble goes out in all directions encompassing all!

## 6 The Three Prophesies

As I write this in early 2011, the world is living out one of its great revealings but it is badly interpreted. There is a prophecy that the world would see an antichrist rise and rule the world. They think the antichrist is a person. Here is another consideration. What is Christ? Love. What is the opposite? Fear! What are most of the people in the world experiencing right now? Total, complete fear! Everywhere! We have lived in fear for most of the last century. We had a slight lull in the 1990s with people beginning to communicate and get together. They worked for peace instead of protesting against war. The people who sponsor fear on the planet didn't like it. So they planted a seed of fear again in early 2000 and nurtured it to what it has become. They created it. I've explained throughout the books who "they" is. So when we become freed of the fear we will awaken and are awakening and taking back the planet.

The Mayans said that at the end of time the machines will attack! They didn't mean the toaster will get up from the counter and burn you. They were talking about specific machines. What we in North America call computers, the rest of the world calls machines. And it's happening. People are communicating through the computer and planning to get rid of the corrupt governments of the world. When that happens, the people supporting the corruption will start to run as well. Also, as I stated in Chapter 4, Technology, the frequency of the wireless wave is attacking us and awakening us. When many more are affected by the wireless wave, it will affect the flow of the universes. Therefore Universal Mind will shut the technology down, some believe by a solar flare, and send us back to a time before this technology, to an age of more traditional value connected to the land, or a time of rebuilding the society. Probably like the 1930s. The earth changes that I mentioned in Book 1 are starting. As my body released the negative energy, my joints healed. So will the earth, unlocking the plates and allowing the continents to be one again. The body of the earth is no different than our bodies. Everything is about flow and there has not been flow for a very long time.

Now the big one. Jesus will return. It might be him reincarnated or it will be someone, somewhere, someday who will teach the people the principles that Jesus taught with truth and no doubt, absolutely no doubt. That person will lead the world to a truly spiritual evolution, just as Jesus himself tried to do 2,000 years ago. But as I explained, it was hijacked.

What was he really doing? Jesus of Nazareth studied the Jewish texts as a child and was taught about the coming of a Messiah. As a boy of twelve, he, his mother and uncle went to Glastonbury, England where his uncle had mines and Jesus studied at the great library of the ancients—one of three in the world at that time. These writings of the ancients told him the truth about everything and carried Jesus towards his goal of total, complete knowing. He studied and practised and had absolutely no doubt about who he was. He never healed. He only evoked people's faith to heal. He went back to Israel and played the role of the messiah totally and completely but it wasn't "the someone" that the synagogues were hoping for. He was there to free the people by telling the truth. Did he not call the Priests and Pharisees vipers (snakes). They were the ones who had him executed to prevent a populous uprising. He sacrificed himself to save the masses from being slaughtered. Not to wash away any sin, because sin is an illusion.

He created leaders to follow him and teach the truth to the masses and it worked for a time. But as I stated before it was hijacked and changed. They were freedom fighters just like all the prophets wanting freedom for all.

They taught that following Jesus' way you would find truth, and in that, the light; not as the church changed it to "I am the way the truth and the light."

None of these things are outside of us. We can understand anything in our experience. The knowledge is in us and the love is in us. Everything I have spoken of here is within and the understanding comes from following our thought, emotion and experiences—on finding the source of light within us. Through all of this, remember that it doesn't matter, because everything that is, was and will be is happening now and it is just a huge game. We humans tend to take everything a little too seriously. It's all in our experience and we can change our experience to what we desire.

The point about the return of Jesus is, it will be a person who teaches the people the truth with no doubt, and they will evolve. As the people evolve the world will change with equity for all.

Until we understand that all is love, everything is love, nothing but love, the problems that we now face will not change. Once this is accepted in the consciousness of everyone on the planet, then we will manifest the love and change our hearts to manifest the changes required.

We will conceive, create and experience what we, the majority, desire. Then the love of all will prevail creating the new heaven on earth. It's all up to us.

The universal truth of love requires no thing, no rules, no laws, no commandments. Just love one another. Love will manifest.

I hope these words serve you well. I have served others my whole life and other lives before. I don't believe that serving others will change in this life. That is my mission, to serve others. To serve myself. It gives me great pleasure. I am Vincent Janic, that is Vincent the Janitor. I have total certainty, peace and love in my life. May this writing bring it to you.

Love to all.


The end.

# Acknowledgements

I have had assistance from my teacher and *Conversations with God* by Neale Donald Walsch. It gave me the basic laws and principals which I knew in spirit and were confirmed in the book. I have left a few other principles aside because they don't serve this purpose. All good books are guides for those who seek enlightenment of the spirit. I am hoping this guides you to the truth of all that you are and leads you to total and complete freedom as it has for me. Being free from fear is your greatest gift.

Thank you,
Vincent Janic

Made in the USA
Charleston, SC
05 November 2011